THE GROWTH OF WORD MEANING

THE GROWTH OF
WORD MEANING

Jeremy M. Anglin

 Research Monograph No. 63
The M.I.T. Press
Cambridge, Massachusetts, and London, England

ISBN 0 262 01033 X

Library of Congress catalog card number: 79-128536

For Lise

Foreword

This is the sixty-third volume in the M.I.T. Research Monograph Series published by The M.I.T. Press. The objective of this series is to contribute to the professional literature a number of significant pieces of research, larger in scope than journal articles but normally less ambitious than finished books. We believe that such studies deserve a wider circulation than can be accomplished by informal channels, and we hope that this form of publication will make them readily accessible to research organizations, libraries, and independent workers.

Howard W. Johnson

Contents

Preface

As the title page indicates, this book is about the development of word meaning. The approach taken to this exceedingly complex problem has been primarily empirical and descriptive. The work to be reported is primarily empirical because its major emphasis lies in the cross-sectional experiments described in Chapters 3 to 5. The systematic developmental trends which reveal themselves in the form of diverging curves constitute the primary message of this book. The work is primarily descriptive because the experiments were designed to provide a fairly detailed picture of *how* the internal lexicon evolves rather than to provide a complete explanation of *why* it evolves. An adequate explanation of the systematic trends reported here would presumably lead to a consideration of the effects of Western culture, particularly its educational habits and its media. This kind of consideration is beyond the scope of the present project.

If such an emphasis on empiricism and description would seem to preclude theory and speculation, then the reader may find this book something of a paradox. Three of the six chapters that follow deal with the theoretical preconceptions that led to the experiments and the theoretical implications that emerged from them. An attempt has been made to suggest why the empirical curves diverge rather than converge, to provide a model of lexical growth that is consistent with the data, to suggest interpretations for certain results that appear somewhat puzzling, and to unify findings from the several experiments by relating them to presumed linguistic habits.

All but one of the experiments reported here were part of my doctoral dissertation, "The Growth of the Internal Lexicon," completed at Harvard University in 1969 under the supervision of George Miller. I would like to take this opportunity to thank Professor Miller for first engaging my interest in the study of language, for providing continued interest and encouragement and, in general, for being a fine teacher and friend. I would also like to thank the other two members of my thesis committee: Jerome Bruner for first pointing out to me the value of the study of developmental trends as a technique for tapping cognitive processes and for many valuable discussions about the thesis in particular and about development and cognition in general; and Roger Brown, whose excellent book influenced much of my own thinking about lexical growth, for kindly agreeing to read the thesis on short notice and to participate as a member of the committee.

I would also like to thank several people at Bell Telephone Laboratories who helped with various stages of the data analysis this past summer. Lee McMahon, who supervised my stay at Bell Laboratories, allowed me a maximum amount of freedom and support for which I am very grateful. Doug Carroll, Jie Jie Chang, Kirk Smith, Mike Wish, and Ernie Rothkopf provided valuable statistical advice. Mrs. Carolyn Brown was not only extremely helpful with various computer programs but also ran the adult group in the first sorting experiment. Finally, I am especially grateful to Steve Johnson for his invaluable assistance in the application of his various inferential and descriptive statistical techniques to my data.

The following people have been most helpful in providing subjects for the various experiments: Mr. Lazear and Mr. Beatty of the Kingswood School in Hartford; Mrs. Sheridan, Miss Billingham, and Mr. McCloud of the Renbrook School in Hartford; Mr. Stevenson of the Oxford School in Hartford; Mr. Dovi and Mr. Rizuto of the Foxlane Middle School in Westchester; Mr. Fury and Mrs. Ames of the Greenacres School in Westchester; Mr. Stemmer of the Scarsdale High School in Westchester; Dr. Janet Greene of the Dalton School in New York; and The Reverend Mother Ruth of St. Hilda's and St. Hugh's School in New York. Miss Alice Fenvessy, Mrs. Lee McMahon, Dr. Ken Kaye and Dr. Thomas Rowland were also very kind to help me entice subjects to participate in the experiments. Dr. Doris Aaronson generously spent a great deal of her time to help recruit subjects for the last experiments reported in the book.

Mrs. Buena Chilstrom was extremely helpful in all stages of the research. I would like to thank Miss Edith Skaar, who typed the first draft and who also provided several valuable criticisms of its first writing. I am very grateful to Miss Jean Clement and Miss Sydney Reid, who have had the laborious job of typing the final manuscript.

Susan Carey and Fred Morrison often provided valuable suggestions concerning earlier versions of this research. Tom Bever, Jonas Langer, Richard Hurtig, John Grinder, and Steve Reder have also made useful comments. I am especially grateful to two people for going over the first draft of this work in detail: Stephen Mackay, who offered several valuable comments concerning its theoretical implications; and Ronnie McDonald, who made a large number of valuable suggestions regarding the style and the format of the final version of this book.

This research was supported in part by the Advanced Research Projects Agency, Grant No. DAHC 15 to The Rockefeller University.

J. M. A.

THE GROWTH OF WORD MEANING

1 The Biases and Their Manifestations

This book is concerned with twenty words. Specifically, it is a report of several experiments designed to tap the growth of the appreciation of the relations that exist among these words as the individual matures from childhood through adolescence to adulthood. Although most experiments described in this book involve the same twenty words, the hope is that interpolation and extrapolation will be possible, that inferences may be drawn from the experiments and applied to the lexicon as a whole.

Like most experimental programs the one reported here is partly deductive and partly inductive in that it involves a blend of preconception on the one hand and willingness to discover on the other. The preconceptions rest in assumptions about adults: how they understand words, how they appreciate lexical relations, and how they view language as a system. These preconceptions are manifest in the selection of tasks, material, and methods of analysis. The willingness to discover emerges from a question about children: How does the child grow to appreciate the words, their relations, and the language in the way that adults do? The preconceptions and their manifestations are the topic of this chapter; the empirical question will be considered in the next.

Preconceptions

At the most general level there are four biases underlying this work, all of which concern the nature of words. While some of these preconceptions may seem rather obvious, it should be realized that alternative views and points of emphasis are possible. Moreover, while others may at first appear somewhat gratuitous the motivation for their description may become clearer in later sections of the book.

The Word as a Container of Meaning

The first bias is that spoken and written words are distinguished from random noises and mounds of ink in that the former possess meaning while the latter do not. There is no consensus concerning the concept of meaning (Creelman 1966). The following remarks are intended to indicate what is and is not implied by the term as it will be used below.

We are not here concerned with the affective or attitudinal meaning described by the authors of the semantic differential as connotative (Osgood, Suci, and Tannenbaum 1957). On the other hand we are not concerned solely with the denotative function of words, for interword relations are as important for us as is reference. Although the meaning of a word is thought to be given largely by such intraverbal relations, no heavy emphasis is placed on the relation defined by contiguity which according to Deese (1965) is the notion that has dominated the study of association and of meaning throughout the history of philosophy and psychology.

Words function in organizing the world of experience to make it conceptually manageable. A word is generic in that it denotes not one but a group of referents (Vygotsky 1962). It is thus a category label (Brown 1958). The word *dog* refers to collies, terriers, and poodles. Even proper nouns are generalizations, conceptual integrations over space and time. The words *Julius Hoffman* refer to a whole series of related sensory experiences. Moreover, words describing nonphysical entities, actions, relations, and qualities are also generalizations in this sense (Brown 1958). The words *beauty*, *buy*, *between*, and *big* have more than one referent, just as do *bed*, *bomb*, and *butterfly*.

When we use a word to denote an object in the world of sense we do so by ignoring certain properties and paying attention to others (Locke 1690). It is precisely by virtue of the fact that we ignore certain properties that a word can function generically. When I classify the object that now sits in front of me as a *book*, I ignore its position, its coloring, its texture, its size, and its particular binding, and I pay attention to the fact that it is a solid object with pages that have writing on them. The properties that I ignore are irrelevant, while the properties to which I attend are criterial (Bruner, Goodnow, and Austin 1956) in my use of the word. The word is thus the embodiment of a concept (Vygotsky 1962). Henceforth the criterial properties will be called the *features* of a word.

The set of features associated with a word represents a large part of its meaning. The extent to which two words share meaning is a function of the intersection of the two corresponding sets of features. Features are roughly similar to what Katz (1966) calls semantic markers. One of the chief differences between Katz's notion and ours is that he emphasizes the distinction between words and semantic markers (Katz 1966, p. 156), while we prefer to emphasize their communality by noting that both words and their features can be expressed by natural language category labels. Thus, partly for reasons of economy, we assume no qualitative difference in the internal representation of words and features.

The Hierarchical Relations among Words

The second bias about words concerns the fact that they are not isolated unrelated entities but rather cohere in a system. A major basis for the organization of words within the lexicon results from the fact that the features of words can often be cast into a hierarchical or nest-like relation (Miller 1969a). A *collie* is a *dog*, a *dog* is an *animal*, an *animal* is a *living thing*, a *living thing* is an *object*, and an *object* is an *entity*. Such class inclusion relations can be represented by tree-like structures with words on twigs and increasingly generic class labels or features on successively higher nodes of the tree (Miller 1967). Such hierarchically organized features are completely redundant; if an entity is a dog it is also necessarily an animal, living, and so on. If two words share a given feature in a nest they will necessarily share all higher-order features within that nest.

Although the hierarchical relation is not the only type of organization that binds words (Miller 1969a) it has been emphasized by both linguists and psychologists. Katz and Postal (1964) recognized the redundant nature of many semantic markers. They suggested that such class inclusion relations be stated at the beginning of their word dictionary for the purpose of simplifying the semantic component of their theory of linguistic descriptions.

Hierarchical structure has probably been stressed even more by psychologists interested in describing the subjective organization of the lexicon than by linguists interested in developing a theory of semantics. Mandler (1967, 1968), Collins and Quillian (1969), and Anderson and Beh (1968) have all stressed the cognitive efficiency that results from such organization. Efficient modes of organizing and remembering material, particularly when it involves the thousands of items of the lexicon, have been emphasized because of the limited span of immediate memory (Miller 1956a, 1956b). Hierarchical organization is attractive as a model since it explicitly and repeatedly involves "grouping or organizing the input sequence into units or chunks," the means proposed by Miller to break "the informational bottle-neck" imposed by that limited memory.

Sentences as a Source of Verbal Concepts

The third bias concerns the source of an individual's appreciation of the features of words. The meaning of a word can be inferred from the utterances and sentences of the language. As Wittgenstein (1953) put it, the language is a word's "original home." While the meaning of a sentence is largely given by the words that make it up, the converse is equally true: the meaning of a word is largely given by the sentences in which it occurs.

There are, of course, other sources from which features can be associated with words. First there is the ostensive definition, which undoubtedly plays a crucial role in a child's appreciation of the first words he comes to understand. Defining by pointing, however, lacks a firm basis by which the word can be fully appreciated as a generalization. There are also many words that will not stand for inspection. Ostensive definitions of *idea*, *some*, *if*, and *during* are impossible. Second, we sometimes learn a word's meaning by resorting to a dictionary. This, however, is not the usual case, and clearly not the most basic. For dictionary construction relies upon the initial extraction of meanings from the language, and dictionary use presupposes the comprehension of the terms making up the definition.

The sentences in which a word occurs are of great importance in the formation of verbal concepts. What is it in the structure of sentences that allows an individual to determine the features of a word? Suppose that one is introduced to a novel word x in the sentence: "The x bought a hat yesterday." Given an acquaintance with the other words in the sentence one can easily infer that x designates a *human*, since nonhumans do not usually buy hats. Other features of the novel word can be inferred from other sentences. Verbal context thus suggests itself as an important factor in the process of meaning acquisition and has been stressed as such by a number of writers (Brown 1958, Deese 1965, Werner and Kaplan 1950).

Similarity of meaning according to this view is systematically related to privileges of occurrence, a notion that has some support from the analysis of the distributional structure of language (Harris 1954). Two words are thought to share meaning to the extent that they share privileges of occurrence. Studies of adult word association support the notion that privileges of occurrence are important in the psychological proximity or, inversely, the distance between two words. Bipolar contrasts or opposites are often the adults' most common responses in the free association task (Deese 1962, 1964, 1965). *Boy* is the most common response to *girl*, *above* to *below*, *laugh* to *cry*, and *rich* to *poor*. Opposites by definition cannot appropriately apply to the same referent at the same time, and they rarely occur in the same sentence. Antonymous responses in the free association task thus seem to violate a Galtonian theory of word association which is based upon the concept of contiguity (McNeill 1966).

Within the system of Katz and Fodor (1963) such responses correlate nicely with the observation that opposites share the same semantic markers except one. For present purposes the point is that opposites can be substituted in many of the same sentence frames. *Boy* can replace *girl* meaningfully in sentences that do not involve reference to sex, the dimension that distinguishes these words.

Consideration of privileges of occurrence in this way "further erases the distinction between grammar and meaning" (Deese 1965). For according to this view the parts of speech — the nouns, the verbs, the adjectives, the prepositions, and so on — which are defined by descriptive linguists in terms of privileges of occurrence (Fries 1952) are actually semantic distinctions as well as syntactic ones. It is not hard to find the semantic correlates of the form classes. Most nouns designate *entities*; most verbs, *processes*; most adjectives, *qualities*; and most prepositions, *relations*. Parts of speech thus appear to correspond to something like Aristotle's semantic categories, the most abstract concepts given in a language. The correlation between syntactic and semantic categories is only rough (Fries 1952) but "though it is less than perfect . . . it would surely be discovered by native speakers if it could be of any use to them" (Brown 1958). The fact that most adult associates are of the same part of speech as the stimulus (Deese 1965) and the fact that confusions in memory tasks tend to be paradigmatic (Anderson and Beh 1968) suggest that the internal lexicon may be organized in terms of form class. Indeed, "lexical markers may be hierarchically organized under form class" (Anderson and Beh 1968).

We have been warned not to be too quick to equate meaning with privileges of occurrence (Miller 1967). But for at least a subset of the sentences of a language the equation has to hold. In 1940 Russell argued that a natural language such as English was, in fact, composed of a hierarchy of languages (Russell 1940). The lowest language in the hierarchy, which he calls the object or primary language, consists only of words that can be defined ostensively and of propositions that refer to specific events constrained by space and time. Higher-order languages include, in addition to the terms of the primary language, what he calls logical words like *some* or *all* that cannot be defined by pointing. The propositions in these languages are statements about words and about languages and hence they are not constrained by space and time. They are generalizations. The difference between the statements "These apples are round" and "Some apples are round" is qualitative.

The point of relevance for this discussion is that if two words can be substituted in sentence frames of higher-order languages, that is, in statements about words rather than about specific referents, then these two words share meaning. If the same predicate can be applied to two words in such statements, then that predicate describes a feature shared by the words. *Apples* and *oranges* are similar in meaning in part because they are both appropriate in frames such as "Some ___ are round."

The Word as a Social Tool

The last bias relates to the fact that a word is a social phenomenon, a part of the culture, and relatively useless unless it means the same thing to different speakers of the language. It is true that a rather arbitrary relation exists between a word and its referent. The word *dog* signifies a certain class of quadrupeds only for those who speak English. Even within a linguistic community there are bound to be idiosyncratic features associated with words, and idiosyncratic bases for their organization (Tulving 1962). But a word is a tool the function of which is to communicate. Unless the relations between words and referents, and between words and words, are roughly the same for the various speakers of a language, unless words are associated with some of the same features for speaker and listener, writer and reader, communication will be impossible and words will not be serving their function.

Manifestations

These four biases show up in the studies in three ways. They have influenced the selection of tasks, the construction of the set of twenty words, and the choice of methods of analysis.

The Tasks

Miller's sorting and Bousfield's free recall tasks are the experimental techniques that resulted in the primary empirical findings to be described in this book. Other tasks have been employed in an attempt to clarify these phenomena. But the choice of the later tasks was a result of the earlier findings, and the reasons for their use should become clear after the data from the clustering studies have been described. In this section, therefore, we shall concentrate on the sorting and free recall procedures.

Miller has described his sorting procedure in a series of papers (Miller 1967, 1969a, 1969b). Typically he gives his subjects a deck of cards with a word and a sense-specifying definition on each card. The subject is required to sort the words into piles on the basis of similarity of meaning. He is allowed any number of piles with any number of words per pile. For each subject an $m \times m$ incidence matrix (where m is the number of words) is constructed showing for every pair of words whether or not they were put into the same pile. The unweighted incidence matrices for each of N judges are then added to form one matrix. In each of its cells there is a number N_{ij} $(0 \leqslant N_{ij} \leqslant N)$ which represents the number of judges who put words i and j together. A measure of the psychological similarity between the two words is given by N_{ij}; reciprocally, a measure of the psychological distance between the two words is given by $N - N_{ij}$. The matrix is then subjected to various kinds of analyses including Johnson's (1968) hierarchical clustering program.

The results of sorting data on 48 common nouns suggested to Miller (1969a) that adult subjects group words by ignoring the features that differentiate the words and by attending to those that the words share. Presumably, some subjects chose to ignore many features and thus grouped many words together; others ignored only a few features and produced small clusters. The sorting task's sensitivity to hierarchical relations is dependent upon such intersubject variability.

By and large the results appeared consistent with a hierarchical model of subjective lexical organization, although paradigmatic and linear organizations may have been operative in some subsets of words. Such features as *object-nonobject*, *living-nonliving*, and *human-nonhuman* appeared to emerge from an intuitive analysis of the data (Miller 1967).

The ease with which the sorting task can be administered to children, its apparent sensitivity to relations among words chosen from diverse sections of the lexicon, and the possibility of interpreting its results in terms of shared features were all factors which argued for its use. However, for reasons that will become clear it was necessary to replicate the major experimental findings with a different task that employs different instructions. For this the free recall technique was chosen.

Bousfield was the first to use the free recall procedure in order to examine clustering (Bousfield 1953). In the original experiment he presented subjects with a randomized list of 60 words made up of 15 animals, 15 names, 15 professions, and 15 vegetables. Immediately following the presentation, subjects were required to recall as many words as possible with no constraints as to order. The major finding was that subjects tended to group their output in clusters that conformed to the four conceptual categories that Bousfield had built into the set of words.

The interpretation of free recall results differs from that of some other verbal learning experiments in that little reliance is placed upon the concepts of contiguity, of reinforcement, or of stimuli and responses, mediated or otherwise (Deese 1965). The subject is often viewed as an active participant in the experiment who deliberately organizes the input (Mandler 1968, Miller 1956) and who makes use of his knowledge of the many relations that exist among the words in his language (Tulving 1968).

In some respects the free recall task can be viewed as the immediate ancestor of the sorting task. In both, subjects are presented with an array of words, and in both, subjects produce word-clusters. Some of the free recall results might well be interpreted in terms of shared features. Bousfield originally interpreted his findings in terms of the activation of superordinates. Thus the occurrence of *dog* and *cat* both activated the superordinate *animal*, with the result that these words were clustered in recall. The point for us is that such superordinates are important features shared by words.

The necessity of such a principle as Bousfield's superordination (and therefore our shared features) in the interpretation of free recall results has been a subject of debate. The question is whether these results might not all be explained in terms of the "relatively simple associative connections" that exist among words (Bousfield, Steward, and Cohen 1964, Cofer 1965, 1966, Postman 1964). While it is clear that some free recall results can be predicted from free association norms (Jenkins and Russell 1952, Rothkopf and Coke 1961), the question as posed, is misleading for two reasons. First, what has been meant by *explanation* in this context has never been clear (Mandler 1968, Tulving, 1968). No adequate theory of free association exists and a correlation between free association and free recall data does not erase the need for an explanation of either. Second, there are clearly instances of clustering in free recall that would not be predicted by free association norms, at least those computed in the usual way (Tulving 1962a, 1962b) some of which appear to be instances of what Bousfield called superordinates, and what we are calling shared features (Marshall 1963).

A variant of the free recall technique has been employed by Bower et al. (1969) to examine the appreciation of the structural relations among words in adults. To one group of subjects they presented a hierarchically organized set of nested categories on a sheet of paper so that the spatial display reflected the structure implicit in the set of words. Superordinates hovered over subordinates which in turn hovered over still lower level categories. To a control group of subjects they presented the same words arranged in the same tree-like formations but in this case the words were scrambled so that the spatial display did not conform to the class inclusion relations that existed among the words. They found that recall was two to three times better for the structured than for the scrambled material. They also found that this effect could not be predicted by associative "guessing." Their interpretation of this phenomenon in terms of the discovery of the rules or principles that relate the words clearly implies the participation of an active subject who brings his preacquired knowledge of the language as a system to bear upon the task at hand.

The Set of Words

For reasons that will become clear, a crucial concept in this work is the degree of abstractness of the equivalence relation between words. Equivalence is said to exist between any two words when they share a feature or a set of features. The term has been borrowed from Bruner and Olver (1963, and Greenfield 1966). *Dog* and *cat* are equivalent because they are both *animals*, *living*, and so on. *Hot* and *wet* are equivalent because they are both *properties of physical objects.*

The relation of equivalence can vary in what we shall call, with a certain degree of trepidation, abstractness. *Abstractness* is a term that has a wide variety of rather vague uses in English, and hence our trepidation. Brown (1958, p. 266) states that the clearest sense of the "concrete-abstract" distinction is given in terms of subordinates and superordinates. According to this definition the superordinate is more abstract than the subordinate, while the latter is more concrete. Thus abstractness is a completely relative term. Within a set theoretic nest of natural language category labels, a particular label can be abstract in relation to some labels and concrete in relation to others. *Dog* is abstract compared to *collie* and concrete compared to *animal*, for the category *dog* includes and extends beyond the category *collie* while the reverse is true for *dog* relative to *animal.*

There are two problems with such a definition of abstractness. The first is that the notion becomes extremely limited; it is defined only for terms that can be arranged in a nest. Thus no statement can be made about the abstractness of a term like *animal* relative to *petunia* in spite of our intuitions. The second problem with such a notion is peculiar to our use of equivalence relations. Again the relation for one word-pair may be compared to the relation for another word-pair only if the two sets of shared features can be arranged in a nest. The problem here is that it is difficult to say a priori what features a word possesses for the "average" speaker of the language. An individual does have strong intuitions about the features he associates with words. But, although he can safely assume that many of his intuitions will be shared by others (Bias 4), he cannot be certain in all cases. These problems necessitate ultimate reliance upon empirical support for a definition of abstractness that is originally based on intuition. Such support will be developed in Chapter 3.

The original selection of words, however, was determined by the writer's intuitions about word-relations and his desire to construct a set of words such that the shared features could be arranged in a nest. The construction of material based on intuition is certainly not unique (e.g., Bousfield 1953, Bower et al. 1969, Marshall 1963). The chosen words are shown in Figure 1.1. There are 6 nouns, 4 prepositions, 5 verbs, and 5 adjectives. These

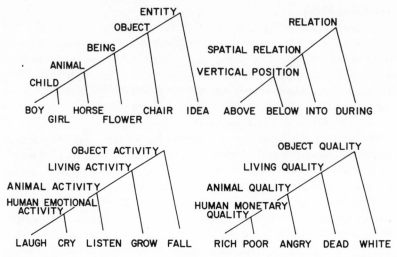

Figure 1.1. Schematic representation of relations among words used in developmental studies.

appear at the ends of the branches of the trees. The hierarchies of concepts that were thought to relate the words have been written in at the nodes.

Consider the nouns. *Boy* and *girl* are both human children. (Of course, *boy* and *girl* are equivalent in that they are both *animals*, *living*, and so on, for, as we have seen, certain features carry with them a host of super-ordinate features. But it is necessary to state only the most concrete feature of a nest since the rest are implied by definition. This most concrete feature will henceforth be called the *presumed minimal feature*. It is presumed because it has been selected entirely on the basis of intuition. It is minimal because it is thought to be represented by the most concrete category label that applies to both words.) *Boy* and *horse* (as well as *girl* and *horse*) are both animals. *Boy* and *flower* (as well as *girl* and *flower*, *horse* and *flower*) are both living organisms or beings. *Boy* and *chair* (as well as *girl* and *chair*, *horse* and *chair*, *flower* and *chair*) are both physical objects. Finally, *boy* and *idea* (as well as *girl* and *idea*, *horse* and *idea*, *flower* and *idea*, *chair* and *idea*) are both entities.

The relations presumed to characterize the prepositions are as follows: *above* and *below* both denote vertical position. *Above*, *below*, and *into* all describe spatial relations. *Above*, *below*, *into*, and *during* all refer to relations, be they spatial or temporal.

Previous attempts by Miller (1969b) to use the sorting technique with verbs and adjectives suggested that subjects tend to group these on the basis of the nouns that accompany such words. Thus the verbs and adjectives are arranged primarily in terms of the nouns that go with them. The five intransitive verbs vary in the type of agent that is capable of performing the action depicted by the verb. *Laugh* and *cry* are both human emotional activities. *Laugh*, *cry*, and *listen* are all animal activities. *Laugh*, *cry*, *listen*, and *grow* are all activities of living things. *Laugh*, *cry*, *listen*, *grow*, and *fall* are all activities of objects, organic or inorganic.

The five adjectives vary in the type of noun they can describe. *Rich* and *poor* are both human monetary qualities. *Rich*, *poor*, and *angry* are all animal qualities. *Rich*, *poor*, *angry*, and *dead* are all properties of things that are living (or have lived). *Rich*, *poor*, *angry*, *dead*, and *white* are all properties of objects.[1]

Figure 1.1 gives only the skeleton of the equivalence relations that exist among these words. Each superordinate or "superset relation" is associated with a host of derivative or "property relations" which constitute the flesh (Collins and Quillian 1969). For example, animals breathe, eat, and move. Thus, *respiration*, *nutrition*, and *motion* all denote relations which make *boy*, *girl*, and *horse* equivalent.

Methods of Analysis

The chosen methods of analysis mirror each of the four biases. Since these reflections will become evident in Chapters 3 to 5 they will be only mentioned here. First, the meaning shared by two words is estimated in terms of the proximity, the major concept of analysis in this work. The proximity for a word-pair is defined by the number of judges who put the two words into the same pile in the sorting task, by the number of subjects who cluster the two words in the free recall task, by the number of responses shared by the two words in the free association task, by the number of individuals who put the two words into the same slot in sentence frames, by the amount of memory facilitation produced by presenting the two words contiguously in a spatial display, or by the number of judges who are able to verbalize a relation that makes the two words equivalent. Second, Johnson's hierarchical clustering program (1967) has been used to depict the appreciation of the class inclusion relations among words. Third, special treatment has been given to clusters comprising opposites and to clusters comprising words of the same part of speech since

---

[1] The features have been chosen to have the property that they are general enough to include every instance of the words over which they hover. If we consider a feature (F) and the words to which it applies ($W_1, W_2, \cdots, W_n$) to be sets then the words have been chosen so that

$$W_1 \, UW_2 U \cdots UW_n \subseteq F$$

these represent the extremes along the continuum defined by privileges of occurrence. Fourth, multidimensional scaling techniques devised by Kruskal (1964), Shepard (1962), and Carroll and Chang (1969) have been used to estimate the extent to which individuals agree in their responses to tasks involving use of the semantic relations among words.

The work is clearly fraught with implicit assumptions that have become explicit as manifestations in three important phases of the experimental program. While empirical confirmation of such assumptions has been an interest, it has not been the only one or even the primary one. The purpose of the next chapter is to describe the nature of the genuinely empirical question at hand, and to suggest that we have got out more than we have put in.

2 The Developmental Question

In Chapter 1 we assumed that for a linguistically competent adult, words are not unrelated entities but rather cohere in a system. The most important threads in an adult's lexical network were there assumed to be determined by features shared by groups of words. This conceptual sophistication of the adult contrasts with the likely ignorance of the infant, at least with respect to the relations among words. There must be an initial period in which words are no more than nonsense syllables, in which they are not associated with features, and in which they do not constitute the highly structured lexical system presumed to characterize the adult mind. Somewhere between birth and maturity such a system evolves. The studies described in this book were designed primarily to tap this evolution.

The Syntagmatic-Paradigmatic Shift

Developmental studies of word association have suggested that an important event in the organization of the lexicon occurs between five and ten years of age (Brown and Berko 1960; Entwisle, Forsyth, and Muus 1964; Ervin 1961; Woodworth 1938). The phenomenon has been called the syntagmatic-paradigmatic shift. It refers to the reliable finding that the responses of young children in free association are predominantly of a different part of speech than the stimulus words (syntagmatic), whereas the responses provided by older subjects are predominantly of the same part of speech (paradigmatic). Thus the most common associate to *table* is *eat* for children but *chair* for adults; the most common response to *dark* is *night* for children but *light* for adults (Woodworth 1938).

13

While syntagmatic responses are often susceptible of interpretation in terms of contiguity, paradigmatic responses are not (Ervin 1961). The one theory that held that paradigmatic responses could be explained by the principle of contiguity has not withstood empirical test (McNeill 1966). The increase in paradigmatic responses can be viewed as reflecting "the accretion of semantic markers" (McNeill 1968) and "the developing organization of vocabulary into syntactic classes" (Brown and Berko 1960), a view which has some support from experiments in short-term verbal memory (Anderson and Beh 1968).

The Polar Hypotheses

It is unlikely that the processes of feature acquisition and of lexical reorganization are completed suddenly. On the contrary, semantic development appears to proceed very gradually (McNeill 1968; Vygotsky 1962). If so, we should be able to examine the process in detail. At the most general level there appear to be at least two opposing views of the nature of lexical growth, either of which is bound to be oversimplified. The first position describes growth as essentially a generalization process in which the child first appreciates the similarity among small groups of words and only later sees the similarity among increasingly broad classes. At first he might see that *roses* and *tulips* are *flowers*, that *oaks* and *elms* are *trees*, that *collies* and *poodles* are *dogs*, and that *diamonds* and *rubies* are *stones*. Somewhat later he might realize that the objects he had classed as *flowers* are similar to the objects he had classed as *trees*, in that both are *plants*. Later still he might form even more general concepts of *living things*, *objects*, and finally, *entities* which would apply to most nouns. Development in the other parts of speech would proceed in a similar fashion.

The validity of the generalization hypothesis was sponsored by Locke (1690):

There is nothing more evident, that the ideas of ... children ... are ... only particular. ... Afterwards when time and a larger acquaintance have made them observe that there are a great many other things in the world, that in some common agreements of shape, and several other qualities, resemble their father and mother, and those persons they have been used to, they frame an idea, which they find those many particulars do partake in; and to that they give with others the name "man," for example. And thus they come to have a general name and a general idea. ... By the same way that they come by the general name and idea of "man" they easily advance to more general names and notions. For observing that several things that differ from their idea of man, and cannot therefore be comprehended under that name, have yet certain qualities wherein they agree with man, by retaining only those qualities and, uniting them into one idea, they have again another and more general idea . . . comprehended under the name "animal" . . . by the same way the mind proceeds to "body," "substance," and at last to "being," "thing," and such universal terms, which stand for any of our ideas whatsoever (Locke 1690, Book III).

More recently Vygotsky (1962) has echoed the same point of view, although less explicitly: "But word meanings evolve. When a new word has been learned by the child, its development is barely starting; the word at first is a generalization of the most primitive type; as the child's intellect develops, it is replaced by generalizations of a higher and higher type" (p. 83); and later, ". . . every new stage in the development of generalization is built on generalizations of the preceding level; the products of the intellectual activity are not lost" (p. 114).

The alternative position envisages lexical growth as essentially a differentiation process, thus joining other theories which view growth as the increasing ability to form finer and finer discriminations (Gibson 1969). According to this view the child first appreciates the very broad semantic distinctions among words, perhaps the semantic correlates of the form classes. *Things* are distinguished from *acts*, *qualities* from *relations*. Growth is accompanied by a gradual differentiation of classes. For example, *things* might be divided into those which are *living* and those which are *nonliving*; later the class of animate objects might be divided into those which are *human* and *nonhuman*. Very fine distinctions are thought to be acquired last.

McNeill (1968) has tentatively suggested that lexical growth proceeds in this way. He describes a major phase of semantic development in terms similar to the ones we have been using. He discusses the "compiling of a word dictionary" in which the child "must begin to build up a system of semantic markers" which he assumes is governed by "a sequential accretion" of features. He then goes on to say, "If we think in terms of distribution classes, that is, words that can appear in the same context, we could say that a child with incomplete dictionary entries has wider distribution classes than an adult. If that is the case, the result of sequentially adding semantic markers should be a narrowing of distribution classes . . ." (p. 7). He offers as a hypothetical example the markers *physical object*, *living*, *small*, and *plant* being added to the dictionary entry for *flower* in that order.

The developmental question referred to in this chapter's title is: Does the individual's appreciation of verbal relations become more abstract as he grows? Although it is a commonplace to describe an adult's thought as more abstract than a child's, Brown (1958) points out that there is, in fact, no substantial evidence to support the thesis of a concrete-abstract progression. The studies reported below were designed to provide some relevant empirical evidence.

The two polar hypotheses espoused by Locke and Vygotsky on the one hand and by McNeill on the other have been clearly articulated and are clearly distinguished with respect to our developmental question. The generalization hypothesis claims that a child's verbal thought becomes more abstract (in the sense of Chapter 1) as he grows; the discrimination hypothesis holds that it only becomes more subtle. Because they are clearly articulated positions we have framed the developmental question in terms of these two extreme views. But as noted above, both positions are oversimplified. The oversimplification shows up in at least three ways.

First, the names *generalization* and *differentiation* themselves are oversimplifications since both processes are involved in either case. To generalize *in the sense that we are discussing* implies a previous differentiation of features. In order to see that *boy* and *girl* are similar (i.e., both *children*) one has to ignore the fact that they are different along the dimension of sex. This requires that the feature specifying sex be sufficiently differentiated from the rest of the concept so that it can be ignored. Similarly the process of differentiation requires previous generalization over a host of concepts. Before the class of *things* can be divided into *living* and *nonliving* one must generalize, in some sense, over the instances of physical objects. We have maintained the terms *generalization* and *differentiation*, for these were used by Vygotsky and McNeill, but the use of either term should not obscure the fact that the other process is involved as a prerequisite.

Second, the equivalence classes involved in the generalization or differentiation processes are probably not totally arbitrary or idiosyncratic. Neither Locke nor Vygotsky nor McNeill specifies what accounts for the accretion of the particular features or the development of the particular classes involved. As pointed out in Chapter 1, the bases for the organization of words have been entrenched in the culture. The society has established a relatively fixed set of such bases which are reflected in its language labels. The variety of potential concepts is infinite. It would be possible to form a disjunctive concept that encompasses only *boys* and *horses* as exemplars. However, society has not chosen to sanctify such a concept with a name of its own. The names that come closest — *animal* or *mammal* — include *boys* and *horses* but extend far beyond them. The equivalence classes that result from either the generalization or differentiation processes presumably conform to these socially accepted classes. Thus, with respect to the process of generalizing, Bartlett (1958) observed: "The great majority of these generalizations are, in fact, taken over ready made, by the thinker, from the society into which he is born" (p. 182). The process of generalization (or differentiation) presumably would not proceed randomly but would take into account the norms of the culture.

Third, two possible meanings of the term *generalization* need to be distinguished. We noted above that the term as we are using it implies differentiation as a prerequisite. The term has been used in some contexts without this implication. Such cases could be viewed as evidence against the notion of a concrete-abstract progression. Roger Brown (1958) reports, on the basis of the diaries of first language acquisition, that the words invented by children are not restricted but rather are often applied to a wide variety of referents. For example, he cites that Wilhelm Stern's son Gunther used the word *psee* for leaves, trees, and flowers, and that Jespersen's nephew applied the word *priest* to his aunt, who happened to be wearing a collar rather like a priest's. Such observations are reminiscent of Watson and Rayner's (1920) classic study in which the child Albert's fear reaction generalized from a white rat to a host of other furry objects. They also accord with Lashley and Wade's (1946) proposal that the dimensions of stimuli do not exist for the organism until that organism has had the opportunity to compare various stimuli differing along the relevant dimensions.

Although such behavior results in flat generalization gradients, it should be distinguished from the generalization process of interest here. The distinction is between generalization referring to a failure to distinguish events that are perceptually similar versus generalization referring to the treatment of discriminably different events as equivalent. This distinction has been made by various authors (e.g., Brown 1958, Skinner 1935). Brown (1958), for example, talks of "abstraction before differentiation" and "abstraction after differentiation." He argues that a child's use of the term *bow-wow* to refer to all quadrupeds does not mean that he has grasped the adult concept. "He generalizes from failure to distinguish dogs from cats from cows from horses. The adult classifies all of these as quadrupeds even though he sees their species and even their individual differences. The adult abstracts from many perceived differences to find a common quality in a single exemplar and generalizes where he has not differentiated. . . . While high abstractions may be a primitive process when they are accomplished in the absence of differentiation they may be an advanced process after differentiation" (p. 286). In our studies we have chosen words which according to Thorndike and Lorge (1944) should be within the vocabularies of the youngest children tested and hence we assume with Miller (1969a) that "all items are conceptually distinct" to all subjects. We are thus dealing with "abstraction after differentiation" and the generalization hypothesis thus becomes a genuinely "empirical form of the thesis of a concrete-abstract progression" (Brown 1956, p. 286).

Relevant Evidence

Although this rendition of the generalization hypothesis is empirical, evidence for its validity has been scanty. Its main support comes from vocabulary studies. In the free association task, children produce fewer superordinate responses than adults (Woodrow and Lowell 1916). In a study designed to compare the vocabularies of children and adults directly, Brown (1957) selected the first thousand most frequent words used by adults from the Thorndike-Lorge list and the first thousand most frequent words from the Rinsland (1945) list for children of the first grade. Nouns found in the list for adults but not in the list for children were often superordinate to those in the list of children. Nouns in the list for children more often depicted referents having visual contour and size than those of adults. Verbs in this list more often depicted animal movement. These studies suggest that children lack the language labels that describe more generic concepts, but offer no guarantee that children do not appreciate such concepts.

Support for the discrimination hypothesis has also been indirect. McNeill (1968) has shown that "five year olds are much less able than eight-year-olds to take advantage of the semantic consistency in sentences" and also that the syntagmatic associates of six-year-old children are anomalous. Although he argues that such findings are consistent with the view "that children younger than eight years appear to have wider distribution classes than adults" (p. 10), he later admits that "we cannot tell from word association itself what semantic markers are present or absent. What we can tell from word association as we can tell from [the semantic consistency experiment] is that a child's dictionary entries remain incomplete well into early school years" (p. 15, 16). On this point both the generalization and discrimination hypotheses agree.

The most puzzling phenomenon for a proponent of the generalization hypothesis is that a child of about four years can speak the language (McNeill 1968). Specifically, the parts of speech are "given proper grammatical treatment" (Brown 1957). In Brown's study nouns and verbs were found to occur in their proper place in sentences of the spontaneous speech of three-to-five-year-olds. In some sense the broad categories that make up the parts of speech are distinct for the child at a very early age. However, "the fact that a speaker observes the syntactical rules that place words in form classes does not alone constitute proof that he detects the semantic correlates of the form classes" (Brown 1958, p. 245).

Nonetheless, a verbal context study carried out by Brown (1957) suggests that some very young children are sensitive to the semantic correlates of the parts of speech. Brown presented three-to-five-year-old preschoolers pictures in each of which a mass noun, a count noun, and an action were represented. For example, one picture showed hands cutting a mass of cloth with a strange tool. Then the children were shown three more pictures, one of each reproducing exactly one of the three salient features of the first picture, the motion, the mass, or the object. Upon presentation of the first picture the experimenter asked them questions which employed a nonsense syllable stem. The nonsense syllables occurred in the question so that an adult could tell whether it referred to a mass noun, a count noun, or a verb. The children were then asked to indicate which of the other three pictures showed an example of the nonsense syllable. For example, if *sib* was to refer to the action the experimenter might say, "Do you know what it means to sib? In this picture you can see sibbing. Now show me another picture of sibbing" (Brown 1957, p. 4).

On the average eleven out of sixteen children picked out the correct picture for the different parts of speech. While 69 percent is not perfect, it suggests that some very young children are in some way sensitive to the fact that count nouns are usually *things*, that mass nouns are usually *substances*, and that verbs are usually *actions*.

Other verbal context experiments that have employed nonsense syllables have not suggested this kind of sensitivity at such an early age. In a study by Brown and Berko (1960) the experimenter introduced a nonsense syllable to a child by using it in two sentences. The sentences were enough to specify to which of six parts of speech the syllable belonged. The children were then asked to guess what it might mean or to use it in a sentence. Only about 35 percent of the responses of children in grade 1 were appropriate. There was a gradual rise of correct responses in grades 2 and 3, but even adults used the syllable properly only 75 percent of the time.

A related study by Werner and Kaplan (1950) also suggests that the child's sensitivity to verbal context develops gradually after the child has started school. They examined children from eight and one-half to thirteen and one-half years of age. They too inserted artificial words into sentence frames so that an adult could infer the meaning of the word. For example, the artificial word *corplum* for which the proper translation was *stick* occurred in sentences such as "A wet corplum does not burn," and "The painter used a corplum to mix his paints." They also found that the younger subjects tested performed poorly, apparently because they often failed to differentiate between the word's meaning and the entire verbal context. Even the oldest groups tested often indicated that for them the word's meaning "bore a wide situational connotation rather than a circum-scribed stable one."

These discrepant findings suggest that presentation and task related dif-ferences are of critical importance in the measurement of a child's sensi-tivity to verbal contexts.[1] When his use of verbal context for inferring the properties of words is supported by visual representation, and when his task is nonverbal as in pointing to a picture, his performance may be appropriate at a very early age (Brown 1957). However, when he is pre-sented with verbal contexts only and not with visual aids, and when his task is to actively extract the meaning of a word so that he can use it in a sentence or define it verbally, his performance may be retarded (Brown and Berko 1960; Werner and Kaplan 1950).

In a study that relates more directly to the work described in the next chapters, Bruner and Olver (1963, and Greenfield 1966) required subjects from ages six to nineteen to verbalize the equivalence relations that existed among groups of words without the aid of visual props. They constructed lists of words which were similar to those of Figure 1.1 in that upon an intuitive examination the relation between successive words appeared to grow in abstractness. For example, one array consisted of the words *banana, peach, potato, meat, milk, water, air*, and *germs*. In an experimen-tal session they would present the first two terms of an array, say *banana* and *peach*, and ask the subject to tell them how these words were similar. They then added *potato* to the list and asked how all three items were alike, and so on.

The ability to generate such equivalence relations increased gradually with age. Particularly germane to the present project was the finding that the younger subjects might give superordinate responses to the first pair or trio of a list but then with the addition of more terms would tend to falter (Bruner, Olver, and Greenfield 1966, p. 77). Such behavior is consistent with the view that for children equivalence relations become more difficult to generate as the relations among words become increasingly abstract. Unfortunately it is also consistent with the view that the ability to gener-ate such relations becomes more difficult as the number of words in-creases.

Bruner and Olver were not primarily interested in the question under consideration here. Had they limited the number of words to two or three for all trials, they would not have been able to tap the various complexive

---

[1] Such findings seem vaguely akin to what Piaget (1954) calls a "décalage" in that they appear to reflect the development of similar cognitive capacities at different ages across the ontogenetic span, although this may be stretching Piaget's intended defini-tion.

structures that appear in the intermediate stages of cognitive growth. It has been necessary to answer our question for ourselves. The last experiment in this project was similar to Bruner and Olver's in that it required subjects to generate equivalence relations for groups of words; it was different in that the number of words per group was always two.

There is no solid empirical foundation upon which we can accept or reject either the generalization or the discrimination hypothesis; the data is either indirect or equivocal. The purpose of the experimental studies described in the next three chapters has been to provide some data to help illuminate the relative validity of the two hypotheses. These studies represent, however, only a beginning.

The Original Sorting Study

The immediate precursor to this research was a study conducted by the writer which has been reported by Miller (1967). In this experiment there were four groups of subjects from grades 3 and 4, grade 7, grade 11, and graduate school (the adults). Each subject was given 36 slips of paper on each of which appeared one of the 36 words which had been used in the study by Brown and Berko (1960).[2] There were 12 nouns, 12 verbs, 6 adjectives, and 6 adverbs in all. The words were quite simple and were presumed to fall within the vocabulary of all subjects tested. The task for each subject was to sort the words into piles on the basis of similarity of meaning. Words which were thought to be similar in meaning were to be put into the same piles. Subjects were allowed to make any number of piles with any number of words per pile.

For each age group matrices were computed showing for every word-pair the percentage of subjects that had put the two words into the same pile. These matrices were then subjected to Johnson's hierarchical clustering scheme (1967). The results of his diameter method program[3] for the adults and for the grades 3-4 children are shown in Figures 2.1 and 2.2. In these graphs gross semantic distinctions are reflected by separate trees. The length of a branch within a tree relates directly to the number of judges who put the words at its end into the same pile.

An inspection of Figure 2.1 reveals that four of the five trees for adults

[2] Actually five of Brown and Berko's words were rejected because they could function in more than one part of speech. These were replaced by words which seemed to the writer to be less ambiguous as to sense.

[3] The diameter method involves an iterative procedure in which the "cluster criterion" is progressively lowered and in which a group of words is considered to have been clustered at a certain level only when each of the possible pairs of words has been put into the same pile the criterial number of times (see Johnson 1967 for details).

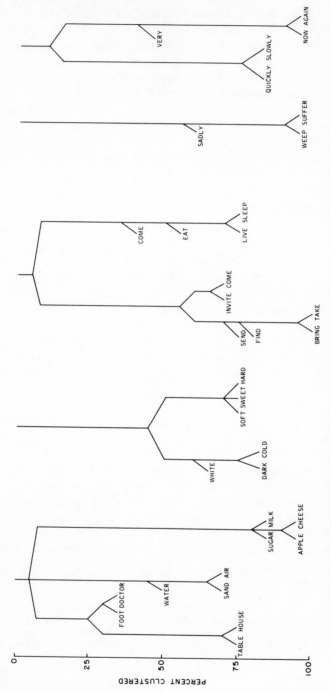

Figure 2.1. Hierarchies from the original sorting experiment for adults: diameter method.

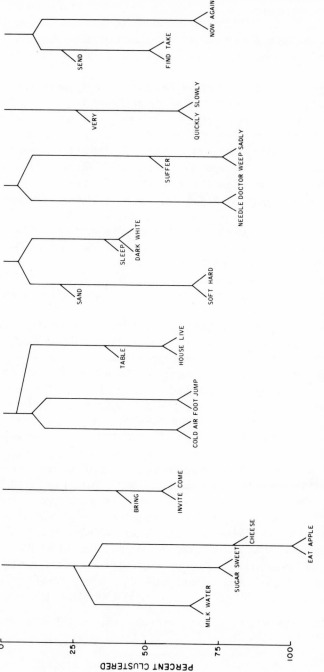

Figure 2.2. Hierarchies from the original sorting experiment for grades 3-4: diameter method.

are made up of words from the same part of speech. One tree contains an adverb, *sadly*, and two verbs, *weep* and *suffer*. With this exception, however, adult judges seem to respect syntactic categories when required to perform a task with instructions that are given entirely in terms of meaning.

The grades 3-4 children, however, tend to ignore the form class distinction that seems so important to adults. In Figure 2.2, which shows the Johnson hierarchies for the children, five out of seven trees include words from different parts of speech. The children's clusters often seem to be based on a thematic or syncretic principle. Thus all of them agree that *eat* and *apple* belong in the same pile. For many of them *air* and *cold* are semantically similar, as are *foot* and *jump* or *live* and *house*. For some, *needle*, *doctor*, *suffer*, *weep*, and *sadly* all belong together as being similar in meaning.

In Figure 2.3 particular word-pairs have been selected as best illustrating the developmental trends that occurred in this classification task. The tendency to cluster words from different syntactic classes – *eat* and *apple*, *cold* and *air* – can be seen to decline systematically with age. The tendency to cluster words from the same part of speech – *bring* and *take*, *live* and *sleep*, and *slowly* and *sadly* – can be seen to increase with age.

There were, however, certain word-pairs from the same part of speech for which the extent of clustering remained fairly high and roughly constant. Among these were the pairs *apple* and *cheese*, and the opposites *hard* and *soft*, and *quickly* and *slowly*, which are shown in Figure 2.4. The point about such word-pairs is that the relation binding them seems relatively specific or concrete. They appear to share many features in common. The fact that these words were clustered equally often by young and old, whereas words that seemed to be more abstractly related were not, lent some support to the generalization hypothesis – to the notion that the construction of the subjective lexicon proceeds from the ground up.

Two other age-related differences that were observed in this study deserve mention. First, adults tended to group more words together than did children. The average number of words per pile was slightly less than three for adults but only slightly more than two for children. Second, the children tended to be somewhat more idiosyncratic than the adults. In order to picture the individual differences in sorting behavior the following analysis was performed. A measure of similarity (Johnson 1968)[4] was calculated for every possible pair of adults and children. These similarity mea-

---

[4] This similarity measure is thought to be roughly independent of cluster size (Johnson 1968).

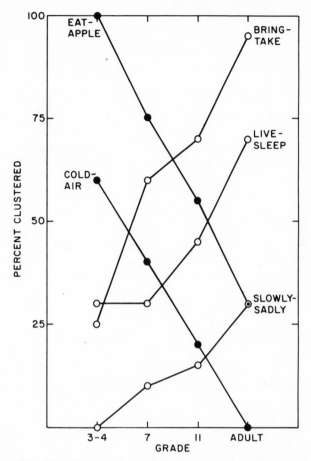

Figure 2.3. Developmental trends in the original sorting experiment.

sures were then applied to the Kruskal-Shepard multidimensional scaling program (Kruskal 1964; Shepard 1962) in which the goal is to produce a configuration such that the interpoint distances are monotonically related to dissimilarity. The two-dimensional plot, which has a stress of 0.23, is shown in Figure 2.5. Adults are represented by X's; grades 3-4 children are represented by O's, a convention that will be followed throughout this volume. Although there are a few exceptions the majority of adults are fairly homogeneous in their sorting and congeal together in the first quadrant of the plot. The children, on the other hand, are more idiosyncratic as evidenced by their being scattered among the other three quadrants.

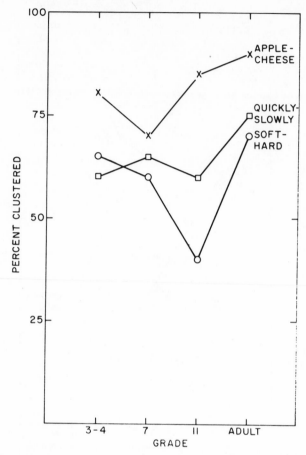

Figure 2.4. Extent of clustering closely related word-pairs in the original sorting experiment.

The Remainder of the Book

The research described in Chapters 3 to 5 was conducted with the results of this sorting experiment in mind. In particular this research explores the reliability, alternative manifestations, and various ramifications of the data in the original experiment, especially those that appeared to lend support to the generalization hypothesis. In Chapter 3 two sorting experiments are reported in which the twenty words of Figure 1.1 were used. Because of the peculiar construction of these words (see Chapter 1) the generalization hypothesis could be tested fairly directly. In Chapter 4 the results of a free recall experiment and of a free association study are reported. These

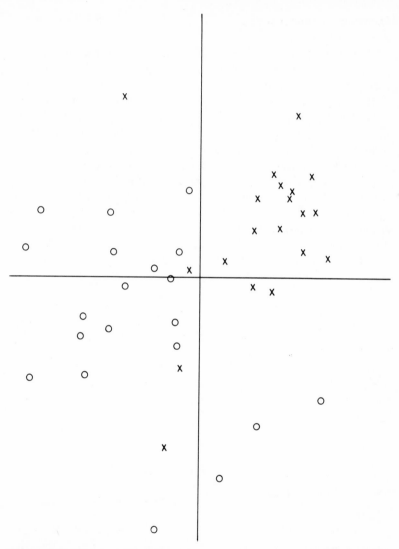

Figure 2.5. The two-dimensional subject space for the original sorting experiment (Kruskal-Shepard).

studies were conducted to see if the sorting findings could be replicated in tasks that do not involve the term *similarity of meaning* in the instructions. In Chapter 5 three experiments are reported in which the goal was to clarify the significance of the systematic trends revealed by the clustering studies. Finally, in Chapter 6 an attempt is made to integrate the findings and to interpret them in the light of the theoretical considerations outlined in Chapters 1 and 2.

There often exists an understandable tendency on the part of a reader to concentrate on the theoretical segments of a piece of work and to neglect the description of experiments. In Chapters 3 to 5 I have tried to keep methodological, technical, and statistical esoterica to a minimum in the hopes that the temptation to skim will not overwhelm the reader. For it is my opinion that the following empirical chapters are the most important in the book. There are three reasons for this opinion. First, they justify, to a certain extent, the theoretical considerations outlined in the first two chapters which otherwise might seem somewhat gratuitous. Second, they suggest the limits as well as the strengths of such considerations. Third, regardless of the validity of the theoretical conjectures, the following three chapters present a number of systematic trends that account for a great deal of the difference between adults and children in their response to verbal tasks. These empirical trends constitute the primary message of the book.

3 The Sorting Experiments

The First Sorting Experiment

The results from two sorting experiments make up the subject matter of this chapter. The purposes of the first experiment were (1) to replicate the results of the writer's original sorting experiment, described in Chapter 2 with the twenty words of Figure 1.1; and (2) to provide the empirical support alluded to in Chapter 1 for the intuitive notion of degree of abstractness.

Method

There were five groups of subjects with twenty males and twenty females per group. The youngest groups consisted of students from the grades 3-4, grades 7-8, and grades 11-12 classes of private schools in Hartford, Connecticut. According to the teachers, about 90 percent of their students go to four-year colleges upon graduation. The fourth group (the college students) was made up of undergraduates, graduate students and their wives, and one research assistant at Harvard University. The fifth group (the adults) consisted of employees at Bell Telephone Laboratories who had previously graduated from college. The median ages for the groups were 9, 13, 17, 24, and 26.5 years, respectively. Each of the three youngest age-levels was tested in groups; subjects in the two oldest age-levels were tested individually.

In an experimental session a subject was handed an envelope in which there were twenty slips of paper that had been previously shuffled. On each slip appeared one of the twenty words of Figure 1.1 with a simple definition to specify the intended sense of the word. The presumed relations among the twenty words have been described in Chapter 1. Nineteen of the words are A and the twentieth, *angry*, is AA (Thorndike and Lorge 1944). Hence, they were all thought to be within the vocabulary of the youngest subjects tested (Thorndike and Lorge 1944, p. xi). The words were chosen so that each functions primarily in one part of speech. Although some of the words may occur in more than one form class the definition was thought to eliminate any ambiguity in this respect.

The subjects were instructed to sort the words into piles on the basis of similarity of meaning. This was elaborated for the younger groups with such statements as "Put the words that are the same in meaning, that mean kind of the same thing, into the same piles." What was meant by similarity of meaning was not specified further for any group. Subjects were allowed to make any number of piles with as many words per pile as they wished.

Questions were answered only for the individual who asked. If one of the younger subjects had a question he raised his hand and the experimenter went and spoke to him quietly. The most common question was whether it was permissible to put the opposites into the same pile. This was asked a few times in each of the age groups. The answer given was always ambiguous: "You may if you want but you don't have to," or "you may if you think they are similar in meaning." Two adults refused to participate in the experiment because of the "ambiguity of the instructions." They were replaced. There was no time limit and subjects spent from five to twenty minutes at the task.

Results and Discussion

Empirical Support for the Notion of Abstractness. Incidence matrices were computed for each of the subjects showing for every pair of words whether or not they had been put into the same pile. The unweighted incidence matrices were then added for all subjects within a group. The resulting matrices were then normalized by dividing each cell entry by the number of subjects (40).

Table 3.1 shows the pooled matrix for adults. Since it is necessarily symmetric, only its lower half is shown. The diagonal cells can be assumed to read 100 percent. In each cell there is a percentage, P_{ij}. P_{ij} refers to the proportion of subjects who put words i and j into the same pile. Thus, for example, 98 percent (39 out of 40) of the adults put *boy* and *girl* together.

The matrix has been organized so that the extent of clustering for the nouns, for the prepositions, for the verbs, and for the adjectives appears in the triangles against the diagonal. Also within a triangle the presumed level of abstractness decreases as one reads down a column. For example, read-

Table 3.1. Matrix Showing Proximities for Word-Pairs Based on Adult Sorting in the First Experiment ($N = 40$).

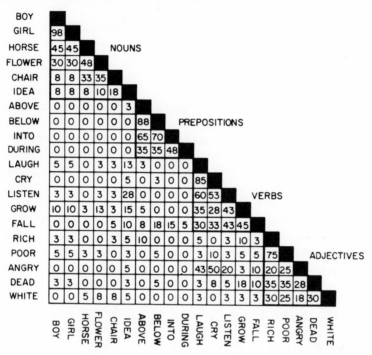

	BOY	GIRL	HORSE	FLOWER	CHAIR	IDEA	ABOVE	BELOW	INTO	DURING	LAUGH	CRY	LISTEN	GROW	FALL	RICH	POOR	ANGRY	DEAD	WHITE
BOY																				
GIRL	98																			
HORSE	45	45																		
FLOWER	30	30	48																	
CHAIR	8	8	33	35																
IDEA	8	8	8	10	18															
ABOVE	0	0	0	0	0	3														
BELOW	0	0	0	0	0	0	88													
INTO	0	0	0	0	0	0	65	70												
DURING	0	0	0	0	0	0	35	35	48											
LAUGH	5	5	0	3	3	13	3	0	0	0										
CRY	0	0	0	0	0	5	0	3	0	0	85									
LISTEN	3	3	0	3	3	28	0	0	0	0	60	53								
GROW	10	10	3	13	3	15	5	0	0	0	35	28	43							
FALL	0	0	0	0	5	10	8	18	15	5	30	33	43	45						
RICH	3	3	0	0	3	5	10	0	0	0	5	0	3	10	3					
POOR	5	5	3	3	0	3	0	5	0	0	3	10	3	5	5	75				
ANGRY	0	0	0	0	0	5	0	0	0	0	43	50	20	3	10	20	25			
DEAD	3	3	0	0	0	3	0	5	0	0	3	8	5	18	10	35	35	28		
WHITE	0	0	5	8	8	5	0	0	0	0	3	0	3	3	3	30	25	18	30	

NOUNS — PREPOSITIONS — VERBS — ADJECTIVES

ing down the left-most column in the noun-triangle we can see cells for the word-pairs *boy-girl, boy-horse, boy-flower, boy-chair* and *boy-idea*. According to the intuitions of Chapter 1 this series of word-pairs was thought to increase in abstractness.

The high density of the triangles means that adults tend to put words of the same part of speech together more often than words of different parts of speech. This is a highly reliable finding.[1] Within a form class they put opposites together more often than other words. In fact, within a given part of speech there appears to be a decreasing tendency to cluster word-pairs as a function of what we have been calling degree of abstractness. The left most column in the noun triangle shows that 98 percent of the

---

[1] The respect ratio (Johnson 1968), a statistic which in this case reflects the percentage of pairs homogeneous with respect to part of speech, was computed for each of the incidence matrices for the adults. The respect ratios were averaged and the resulting mean was compared to the mean expected if the sorting had been random. Adults were clearly sorting according to part of speech more than would be expected by chance ($Z = 8.26$, $p \ll 0.001$).

subjects put *boy* and *girl* together, 45 percent put *boy* and *horse* together, 30 percent put *boy* and *flower* together, and only 8 percent put *boy* with *chair* or *boy* with *idea*.

The left-most column in the preposition triangle is similar. Eighty-eight percent put *above* with *below*, 65 percent put *above* with *into*, and only 35 percent put *above* with *during*. In the case of the verbs the trend is 85, 60, 35, and 30 percent for the pairs *laugh-cry*, *laugh-listen*, *laugh-grow*, and *laugh-fall*. One percentage is out of line in the left-most column for the adjectives. Seventy-five percent put *rich* with *poor*, only 20 percent put *rich* with *angry*, 35 percent put *rich* with *dead*, and 30 percent put *rich* with *white*. Apparently, some adults preferred to cluster *angry* with the verbs *laugh* (43 percent) and *cry* (50 percent) rather than the other adjectives. This may well reflect the kind of context effect that Susan Carey has been studying (personal communication).

The other columns within the part of speech triangles also tend to decrease as the relative number of features presumed to be shared by two words decreases. Only three out of forty-one cells within the columns would have to be changed to generate a perfect monotonically nonincreasing fit between the tendency to cluster two words and our intuitively defined notion of degree of abstractness.

With the exception of the adjectives there does seem to be a slight tendency for the percentages to rise as the rows within a part of speech are read from left to right. The most striking example of this appears in the fifth row of the matrix. *Chair* is put with *boy* and with *girl* only 8 percent of the time. However, *chair* is put with *horse* by 33 percent and with *idea* by 35 percent of the adults. This horizontal drift was not expected. There is reason to believe that it is partly an artifact[2] and the matrix of proximities for the second sorting experiment shows no such effect while it shows an even more systematic vertical decline than Table 3.1. Even in Table 3.1 the vertical effect is clearly larger and more consistent than the horizontal one.

The vertical effect is not surprising. It simply supports our suspicions about the relative number of shared features of the various word-pairs in view of Miller's (1969a) interpretation of sorting results. Nonetheless, this effect does provide the required empirical grounds for maintaining the intuitively defined notion of degree of abstractness. In spite of the slight

---

[2]Most adult subjects were observed first to cluster words for which the relations were thought to be concrete. For example, an adult might put the prepositions *above* and *below* into the same pile. Then some adults who seemed not to like to leave any words single, would group other word-pairs like *into* and *during* almost as an afterthought.

horizontal shift noted above, in Figure 3.1 we have averaged the entries within a given row of a triangle to make these empirical grounds picturable. Figure 3.1 shows that within a given part of speech the extent to which adults cluster two words decreases with the level of abstractness that was presumed to bind them in Chapter 1. Consider the nouns. Ninety-eight percent of the adults put the words that both referred to children, *boy* and *girl*, into the same pile. On the average, 45 percent of the adults clustered word-pairs for which the presumed minimal feature was *animal*. These were *boy-horse* (45 percent) and *girl-horse* (45 percent). An average of 36 percent clustered the word-pairs for which the presumed minimal feature was *being*. These were *boy-flower*, *girl-flower*, and *horse-flower*. The function for nouns continues to decrease as the generality of the presumed minimal feature shared by words increases.

The curve for prepositions, constructed in the same way, is also a

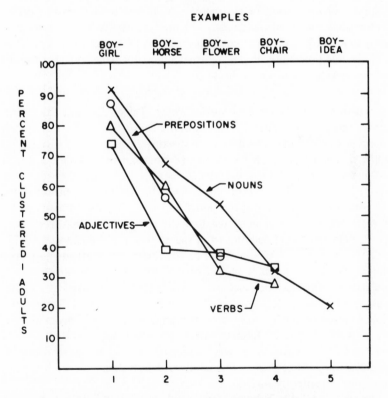

Figure 3.1. Extent of clustering for adults in the first sorting experiment as a function of the presumed level of abstractness.

monotonically decreasing function of the presumed level of abstractness. The curves for the verbs and adjectives are also decreasing but they are not monotonic. There is one point out of line for each. Table 3.1 shows that adults tended to put *fall* with *grow* (vertical motion?) and with *listen* more often than predicted. The previously noted tendency to put the adjective *angry* with the emotion verbs *laugh* and *cry* probably accounts for the deviant point in the adjective curve. With these two exceptions, however, the extent of clustering decreases with the presumed number of shared features. (It should be noted that, although the abscissa has been divided into equally spaced intervals, only an ordinal relation is assumed; the points have been connected by lines only as a visual aid. This will be true for many of the graphs to follow.)

The validity of Miller's sorting theory is assumed and thus, in spite of the two discrepancies, Figure 3.1 is interpreted as general empirical confirmation of the intuitive definition of abstractness. This analysis thus shifts the emphasis in the notion of abstractness from nested categories to shared features. Of course, in the words of Figure 1.1 these two are presumed to be redundant. But the shift in emphasis allows for a degree of verifiability and also the possibility of gauging abstractness for words whose relations cannot be arranged in a nest. These points will be raised in Chapter 6.

Comparison with the Original Sorting Study. Table 3.2 shows the matrix for the grades 3-4 children. Once again the density of the part of speech triangles suggests that children are respecting the form-class distinction. While this is a highly reliable finding ($Z = 6.19$, $p \ll 0.001$) it is not as striking as in Table 1 for the adults. A measure of the distance (Johnson 1968) between each observed clustering and a theoretical clustering into the four parts of speech was computed for every adult and for every child. A Mann-Whitney U test indicated that the adults' clusterings were more like the clusterings defined by part of speech than the children's ($Z = 3.77$, $p < 0.001$). This finding appears to be the result of two effects. First, the children tended to produce smaller clusters than did the adults ($Z = 3.53$, $p < 0.001$). This can be seen by comparing the two matrices. On the whole, entries in Table 3.2 are smaller than those in Table 3.1. Second, the child's clustering tended to be more syntagmatic or heterogeneous according to part of speech. Respect ratios, for which the expected value is independent of cluster size, were compared for adults and children. A Mann-Whitney U test showed that adults respect the part of speech distinction more consistently than do children ($Z = 2.55$, $p < 0.01$).

Inspection of Table 2 shows that the only word-pairs that most children cluster together are the opposites. These they treat much as do the adults.

Table 3.2. Matrix Showing Proximities for Word-Pairs Based on Grades 3-4 Sorting in the First Experiment ($N = 40$).

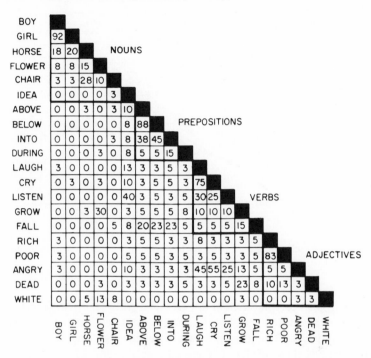

	BOY	GIRL	HORSE	FLOWER	CHAIR	IDEA	ABOVE	BELOW	INTO	DURING	LAUGH	CRY	LISTEN	GROW	FALL	RICH	POOR	ANGRY	DEAD	WHITE
BOY																				
GIRL	92								NOUNS											
HORSE	18	20																		
FLOWER	8	8	15																	
CHAIR	3	3	28	10																
IDEA	0	0	0	0	3															
ABOVE	0	0	3	0	3	10														
BELOW	0	0	0	0	0	8	88		PREPOSITIONS											
INTO	0	0	0	0	3	8	38	45												
DURING	0	0	0	3	0	8	5	5	15											
LAUGH	3	0	0	0	0	13	3	3	5	3										
CRY	0	3	0	3	0	10	3	5	5	3	75									
LISTEN	0	0	0	0	0	40	3	5	3	5	30	25		VERBS						
GROW	0	0	3	30	0	3	5	5	5	8	10	10	10							
FALL	0	0	0	0	5	8	20	23	23	5	5	5	5	15						
RICH	3	0	0	0	0	3	5	5	3	3	8	3	3	3	5					
POOR	3	0	0	0	0	5	5	5	3	5	3	5	3	3	5	83		ADJECTIVES		
ANGRY	3	0	0	0	0	10	3	3	3	3	45	55	25	13	5	5	5			
DEAD	0	0	0	3	0	3	3	3	3	5	3	3	5	23	8	10	13	3		
WHITE	0	0	5	13	8	0	0	0	0	0	0	0	0	3	0	0	0	3	3	

In fact, the tendency to cluster opposites was high and fairly constant for the five age groups. The tendency to cluster words from the other parts of speech can be seen to be less for the grades 3-4 children than for the adults. In fact the tendency to cluster words of the same part of speech other than opposites increased with age on the average, although quite gradually. Figure 3.2 shows these effects for the opposites and for one other pair for each of the four parts of speech. The curves for the opposites are high and remain fairly flat as a function of age. The functions for examples from the other parts of speech start much lower and can be seen to rise gradually with age.

The matrices in Tables 3.1 and 3.2 were subjected to Johnson's hierarchical clustering program (1967) and the results of the diameter method are shown in Figures 3.3 and 3.4. Each of the four trees in Figure 3.3 for the adults consists entirely of one part of speech. Moreover, the resulting hierarchies resemble the theoretical trees of Figure 1.1. There are three discrepancies between the adults' trees and the theoretical ones. These include (1) the fact that *boy* and *girl* are on a branch that is separate from

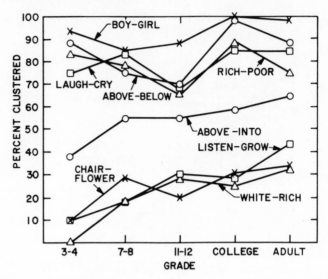

Figure 3.2. Developmental trends in the sorting of words from the same part of speech.

the other physical objects; (2) the fact that *grow* and *fall* have been grouped by almost half the subjects; and (3) the fact that *angry* appears at a relatively low level on its tree. By and large, however, adults do conform to the theoretical hierarchies of Figure 1.1.

The trees shown in Figure 3.4 which were produced by the grades 3-4 children contrast markedly with those of the adults. Only one of the four trees is homogeneous by part of speech, the one containing the opposites *boy* and *girl*. The remaining trees all contain words from different parts of speech. There seems to be a mild tendency to produce clusters of words the relation among which might be called thematic. Such clusters are *flower* and *grow*, *idea* and *listen*, *angry*, and *laugh* and *cry*. This tendency is weak, however.

In fact, there are no striking examples of a decline with age in the tendency to cluster words which appear to be bound by thematic relations. This is one respect in which this study differs from the original developmental sorting experiment.

Individual Differences. Another inconsistency between the two experiments concerns intersubject variability among the adults and among the children. In the original study adults were found to be more consistent with one another in their clusterings than were children. To estimate the

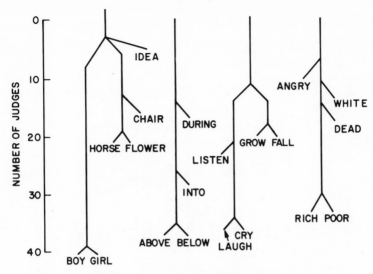

Figure 3.3. Sorting hierarchies for adults: diameter method.

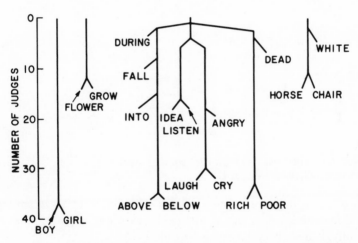

Figure 3.4. Sorting hierarchies for grades 3-4: diameter method.

group conformity in the present experiment we computed a measure of similarity for each of the 3,160 possible pairs of adults and children. (This measure was the same as was used for the original sorting data.) These similarity measures were then fed into the Kruskal-Shepard multidimensional scaling program. The two-dimensional plot (which has a stress of 0.27) is shown in Figure 3.5. Although there does seem to be some separa-

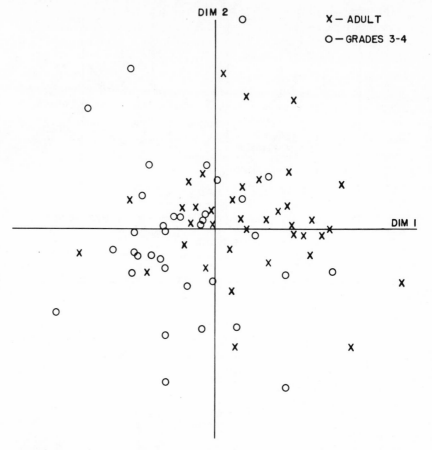

Figure 3.5. The two-dimensional subject space for the first sorting experiment (Kruskal-Shepard).

tion of the two groups of subjects, this separation is by no means complete. Moreover, adults appear to have behaved only slightly more consistently, if at all, than the grades 3-4 children.

Conclusions

By and large the intuitions upon which the set of twenty words was constructed have received empirical support. Adults often cluster words the relations among which were presumed to be concrete whereas they seldom cluster words for which the relations were presumed to be abstract. The result is a shift of emphasis in our notion of abstractness from nested categories to shared features (Miller 1969a).

The major findings of the original developmental sorting experiment have been replicated. Adults' clusters conform to the distinction based on part of speech more than do children's; children's clusters are smaller and more syntagmatic. Within a given part of speech, children tend to group opposites as often as do adults, whereas they group other words of the same form class less often. There were, however, two discrepancies between this experiment and the original. There were no striking examples of the decline with age in thematic groupings. Moreover, the original finding that children's clusterings were idiosyncratic relative to adults' was not replicated.

These discrepancies are thought to be related in part to the tendency, particularly noticeable among young children, to produce very small clusters. For example, five of the grades 3-4 subjects grouped only the opposites and left the rest of the words single. The point is that the combination of such small clusters and the uniformity toward opposites precludes the possibilities of great intersubject variability and of strong thematic clusters. The second sorting experiment forced subjects to make large clusters to get around this problem.

The Second Sorting Experiment

The first experiment was necessary to support the notion of abstractness and to verify that sorting is a valid technique for getting at the development of verbal relations. The main purpose of the second experiment was to examine this development in detail. In this study we have required all groups of subjects to make very broad clusters — to sort the twenty words into exactly four piles. In terms of Miller's theory we are forcing subjects to ignore several features that distinguish the words, and thus to make use of abstract relations. A secondary purpose has been to generate word hierarchies for individual subjects to be compared with the group trees.

Method

There were four groups of subjects with twelve males and twelve females per group. The three youngest groups consisted of students in the grades 3-4, grades 7-8, and grades 11-12 classes of the same private schools which had provided subjects for the first experiment. No individual served in both experiments, however. The fourth group, which we shall now call the adults, consisted of undergraduates and graduate students from Harvard and Radcliffe. The median ages for the groups were 9, 13, 17, and 20 years, respectively. All subjects were tested individually.

Each experimental session was divided into two parts.

Part 1: The first part was similar to the first sorting study except that subjects were required to sort the words into exactly four piles on the basis of similarity of meaning, rather than into as many as they wished. Once again there was no time limit and subjects typically spent from five to twenty minutes at the task.

Part 2: In the second part, subjects in each age group were divided into two subgroups equally balanced for sex. An individual in the first subgroup was required to reject from each pile the word that was least similar in meaning to the rest of the words in its pile. Then he was required to reject the word which least belonged in the remaining piles, and so on until there were only two words in each pile. An individual in the second subgroup was required to indicate which two words in each pile were most similar in meaning. Then for each pile he was required to indicate which word was next most similar to the corresponding word-pair which he had just selected, and so on until there was only one word left in each pile. Again subjects could take as long as they liked in their selections. This part of the task required about ten minutes per subject.

After the experiment subjects were asked if they knew what the term *parts of speech* meant and if they had ever heard of nouns, verbs, adjectives, and prepositions. If they indicated such knowledge they were given the set of twenty words again and asked to sort them according to part of speech into four piles: one for the nouns, one for the verbs, one for the adjectives, and one for the prepositions.

Results and Discussion

A Close Look at Developmental Trends in Sorting. Data from the two parts of the experiment were analyzed separately.

Part 1: Incidence matrices were constructed for each subject showing which word-pairs he had grouped in his choice of four piles. These were then added to form matrices showing how often word-pairs had been clustered by the twenty-four subjects in each age group. Adults again tended to respect the part of speech distinction ($Z = 6.9, p \ll 0.001$). Although children also sorted somewhat according to part of speech the effect was not nearly so marked ($Z = 2.10, p < 0.02$). A Mann-Whitney U test showed that adults respected the distinction significantly more than did the children ($Z = 4.08, p < 0.001$).

A more detailed comparison of the differences in sorting with respect to parts of speech is given in Figures 3.6-3.10 which depict the major empirical findings of this chapter. Figure 3.6 shows for the different age groups the average percentage of noun-pairs clustered as a function of the generality of the minimal feature presumed to bind them. That is, as in

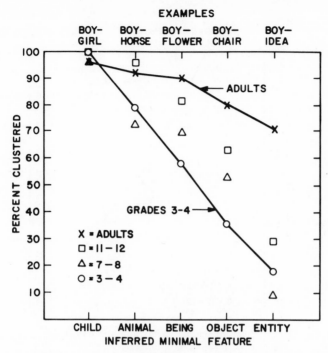

Figure 3.6. Extent of noun clustering as a function of the generality of the relation between nouns for the different age groups.

Figure 3.1, we have computed the degree of clustering for word-pairs which were presumed to have the minimal feature child (*boy-girl*), animal (*boy-horse* and *girl-horse*), being (*boy-flower*, *girl-flower*, *horse-flower*), object (*boy-chair*, *girl-chair*, *horse-chair*, *flower-chair*), and entity (*boy-idea*, *girl-idea*, *horse-idea*, *flower-idea*, *chair-idea*) for each of the age groups. All of the grades 3-4 children put *boy* and *girl* into the same pile. Thus Figure 3.6 shows that the children (represented by O's) clustered 100 percent of the word-pairs with the minimal feature *child*. Nineteen children combined *boy* with *horse* and nineteen combined *girl* with *horse*. Thus Figure 3.1 shows that an average of 79 percent of all possible word-pairs with the minimal feature animal was grouped by these children as being similar in meaning. The other points represent similar calculations.

The fact that the adult curve decreases slightly as a function of the generality of the presumed minimal feature simply suggests again the validity of the intuitions upon which the words were selected, in view of Miller's interpretation of sorting results. The more important finding con-

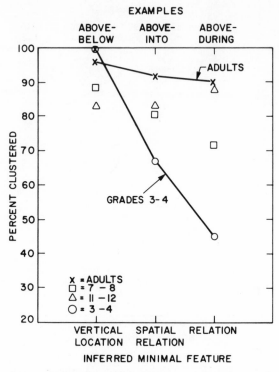

Figure 3.7. Extent of preposition clustering as a function of the generality of the relation between prepositions for the different age groups.

cerns the relation between the curve for adults and the curve for children. These two curves diverge as the presumed minimal feature becomes more general. The children tend to cluster the opposites together as often as do adults. However, the more general the relation between the two words, the greater the difference between the extent of clustering by adults and of clustering by children. The difference, in fact, increases monotonically. In most cases the points for the grades 7-8 and 11-12 subjects fall between these two curves.

Figure 3.7 shows a comparable effect for the prepositions. Again the difference between the extent of clustering for adults and for children increases monotonically with the presumed generality of the relations between prepositions. Figure 3.8 and 3.9 show similar effects for the verbs and the adjectives. However, in neither case does the difference increase monotonically. In each, one difference is out of line. These correspond to

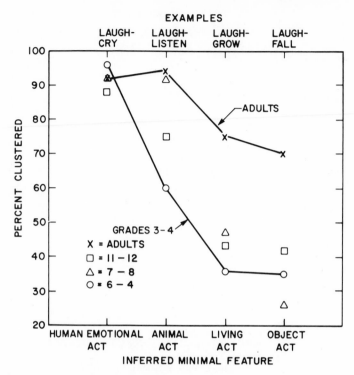

Figure 3.8. Extent of verb clustering as a function of the generality of the relation between verbs for the different age groups.

the two discrepancies noted in Figure 3.1. In this instance the empirical definition of abstractness appears to predict more accurately than the intuitive one. Figure 3.10 is a somewhat artificial representation of the same effect averaged over all parts of speech.

Figures 3.6-3.10 are consistent with the generalization theory of lexical growth. The tendency of children to group opposites as often as adults do suggests that they grasp the specific features associated with words and appreciate concrete equivalence relations. The fact that the difference between the extent of word grouping by adults and by children grows systematically with the generality of the presumed relation between words suggests that children do not appreciate, or at least use, in the way that adults do, the more general features that help define lexical entries.

Figure 3.11 shows that the tendency to group words from different parts of speech such as *angry* and *laugh*, *grow* and *dead*, *girl* and *grow*, and *white* and *flower* systematically decreases with age in this study.

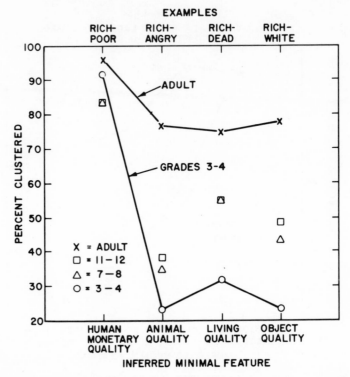

Figure 3.9. Extent of adjective clustering as a function of the generality of the relation between adjectives for the different age groups.

Part 2: Matrices for each subject were computed on the basis of his divisions and subdivisions in Part 2 of the experiment.[3] These were then added for all individuals in a group and the result was normalized by dividing each cell entry by the number of subjects (24).

The matrix for adults is shown in Table 3.3. It has been provided mainly for comparison with Table 3.1, the adult matrix from the first sorting experiment. The main features of Table 3.1 have been replicated in

[3] Individual matrices were computed in the following way. Cell entries were 0 for words i and j if they were not sorted together in the initial division into four piles. For Group 1 cell entries for the two words remaining at the end of a subject's divisions read 1. Cell entries involving either of the members of this pair and the last word to be rejected read $(m - 2)/m - 1$ where m was the number of words in the pile. Cell entries involving any of these three words and the second last word to be rejected read $(m - 3)/m - 1$, and so on. For Group 2 cell entries for the first two words to be selected read 1. Cell entries for either of these and the next word to be selected read $(m - 2)/m - 1$, and so on.

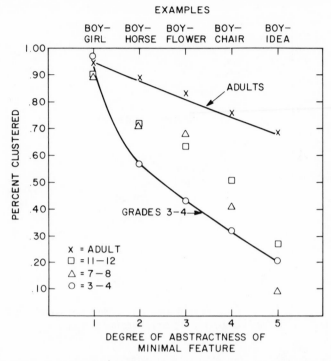

Figure 3.10. Extent of clustering as a function of the generality of the relation between words averaged over parts of speech.

Table 3.3. The cells in the part of speech triangles are clearly denser than the other cells of the matrix. The opposites are the words with the greatest proximities. In the columns of the triangles only two cell entries would have to be changed for a perfect monotonically decreasing relation between the extent of clustering of a word-pair and the degree of generality of the presumed minimal feature. Table 3.3 does not show the systematic horizontal drift effect noted in Table 3.1. As one reads across the rows of the triangles the percentages are more stable.

Figure 3.12 is analogous to Figure 3.1 in that it shows the way the average proximity for word-pairs changes as a function of the presumed level of abstractness. The curves for all parts of speech are monotonically decreasing. Table 3.3 and Figure 3.12 can be taken as further empirical support for the intuitively based notion of abstractness.

Table 3.4 shows a matrix for the children that has been constructed in the same way as Table 3.3. The cell entries for the opposites are roughly the same in both tables. However, in Table 3.4 other entries in the triangles

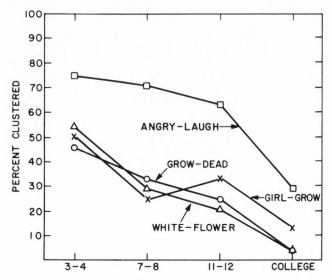

Figure 3.11. Some trends for words of different parts of speech.

Table 3.3. Matrix Showing Proximities for Word-Pairs Based on Pooled Adult Data from the Second Sorting Experiment ($N = 24$).

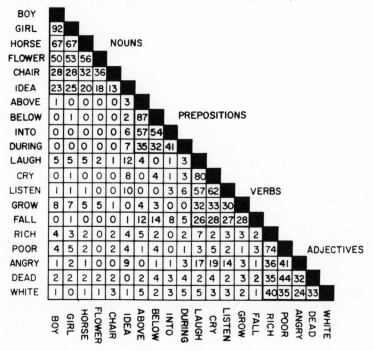

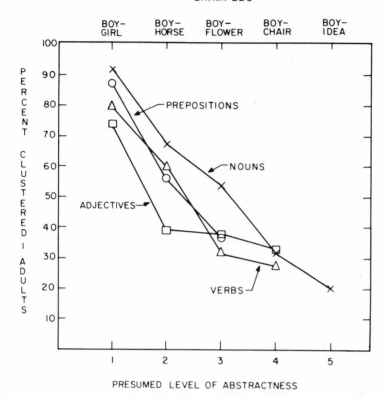

Figure 3.12. Extent of clustering for adults in the second sorting experiment as a function of the presumed level of abstractness.

tend to be smaller and the entries for word-pairs which are heterogeneous by part of speech tend to be larger than the corresponding entries in Table 3.3.

The matrices of Tables 3.3 and 3.4 were subjected to Johnson's hierarchical clustering program. The results are shown in Figures 3.13 and 3.14. Figure 3.13 shows the trees for adults. If the very weak connection between the two branches to the far right of Figure 3.13 is ignored, it can be seen once again that the four major semantic distinctions for adults correspond to the four parts of speech. Within three of the parts of speech, the nouns, prepositions, and verbs, there is a perfect ordinal relation between the extent of clustering of the words and the theoretical trees of Figure 1.1. The deviation in the adjectives shows up in Figure 3.13 as a tendency to cluster *dead* and *white* more often than predicted. An inspec-

Table 3.4. Matrix Showing Proximities for Word-Pairs Based on Pooled Grades 3-4 Data from the Second Sorting Experiment (N = 24).

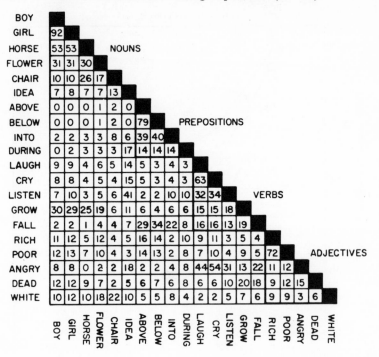

	BOY	GIRL	HORSE	FLOWER	CHAIR	IDEA	ABOVE	BELOW	INTO	DURING	LAUGH	CRY	LISTEN	GROW	FALL	RICH	POOR	ANGRY	DEAD
GIRL	92																		
HORSE	53	53																	
FLOWER	31	31	30																
CHAIR	10	10	26	17															
IDEA	7	8	7	7	13														
ABOVE	0	0	0	1	2	0													
BELOW	0	0	0	1	2	0	79												
INTO	2	2	3	3	8	6	39	40											
DURING	0	2	3	3	3	17	14	14	14										
LAUGH	9	9	4	6	5	14	5	3	4	3									
CRY	8	8	4	5	4	15	5	3	4	3	63								
LISTEN	7	10	3	5	6	41	2	2	10	10	32	34							
GROW	30	29	25	19	6	11	6	4	6	6	15	15	18						
FALL	2	2	1	4	4	7	29	34	22	8	16	16	13	19					
RICH	11	12	5	12	4	5	16	14	2	10	9	11	3	5	4				
POOR	12	13	7	10	4	3	14	13	2	8	7	10	4	9	5	72			
ANGRY	8	8	0	2	2	18	2	2	4	8	44	54	31	13	22	11	12		
DEAD	12	12	9	7	2	5	6	7	6	8	6	6	10	20	18	9	12	15	
WHITE	10	12	10	18	22	10	5	5	8	4	2	2	5	7	6	9	9	3	6

NOUNS · PREPOSITIONS · VERBS · ADJECTIVES

tion of Table 3.3 reveals, in fact, that, within the adjectives the opposites were clustered most often, but the differences between the extent of clustering for other adjective-pairs were minimal.

Figure 3.14 shows the hierarchies for children. There are two large trees, both of which are heterogeneous by part of speech. *Fall* has been grouped with the prepositions, *listen* with *idea*, *angry* with *laugh* and *cry*, *grow* with *dead*, and *white* with *chair*.

Individual Differences. Trees were constructed for each subject based upon his divisions and subdivisions. Although the trees for most adults appeared quite similar to one another, no child could be called typical. Figure 3.15 shows the trees for two adults and two children. J. C. is of interest because, apart from the opposites, his groups and subdivisions tend to be difficult to interpret. This is true of many of the youngest subjects. L. S. is of interest because she seems to be more adult-like in her groupings and subdivisions, at least for words the relations among which are concrete. J. V. is an adult whose initial groupings conform, with one exception

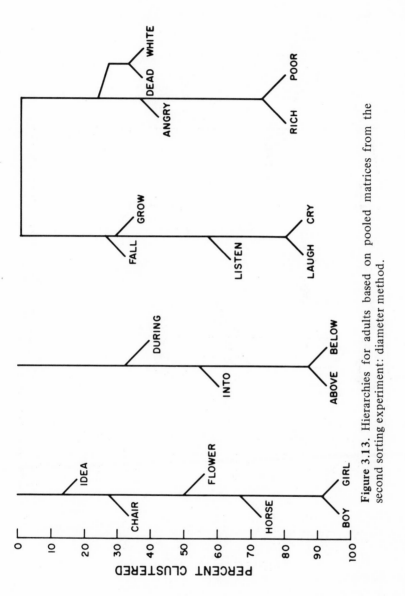

Figure 3.13. Hierarchies for adults based on pooled matrices from the second sorting experiment: diameter method.

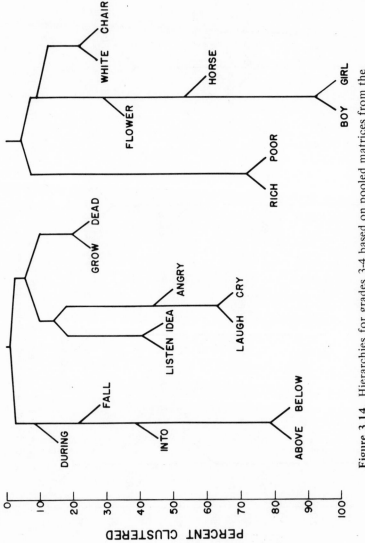

Figure 3.14. Hierarchies for grades 3–4 based on pooled matrices from the second sorting experiment: diameter method.

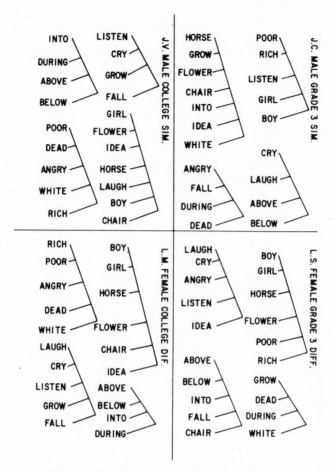

Figure 3.15. Individual sorting hierarchies.

(*laugh* is in with the nouns), to the parts of speech. However, his subdivisions do not reflect the hierarchical structure of Figure 1.1. In this respect he is atypical for his group. L. M. has produced trees identical to those of Figure 1.1. Over half of the adult subjects produced trees that appeared rather similar to those of L. M.

To examine intersubject variability more objectively we have used a program (Carroll and Chang 1969) which has been devised specifically to depict individual differences. The input to the program consisted of the individual matrices for the adults and the children. The output consisted of two scaling solutions which in this case were both two-dimensional. The first solution was a *word-space* which showed how the "average" subject reacted to the words. The second solution, the *subject-space*, gave a configuration of points that reflected the extent to which each individual subject respected the two dimensions of the first space. The two-dimensional word space looked roughly as though subjects who were high on the first dimension had distinguished the nouns from the other parts of speech, and subjects high on the second dimension had separated the prepositions from the nouns and adjectives, and the verbs from all of these.

Thus, as a first approximation, a subject high on both dimensions was one who had respected the part of speech distinction. Figure 3.16 shows the two-dimensional subject space for the adults and the grades 3-4 children. Although these two dimensions account for only about 38 percent of the variance in the data, according to Carroll and Chang the following points should be made about Figure 3.16: (1) The adults tend to be higher on both dimensions which reflects that they tend to cluster more according to part of speech than do the children. (2) A few adults behave like children and a few children behave like adults but by and large there is a

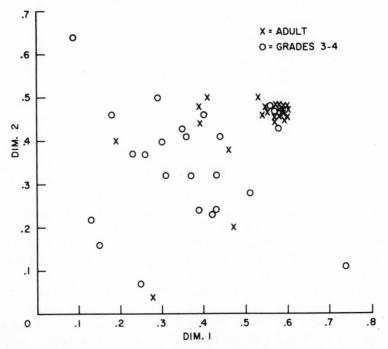

Figure 3.16. The two-dimensional subject space for the second sorting experiment (INDSCALE).

clear separation of the two groups. (3) Adults are more homogeneous in their sorting behavior while children are more idiosyncratic.

Understanding the Concept of Parts of Speech. When the grades 3-4 children were asked if they had heard of nouns, verbs, adjectives, and prepositions, most of them said that they had. However, none of them were able to sort the words according to part of speech. Only 8 out of 24 of the grades 7-8 students were able to sort the words into the four correct piles. Eighteen out of 24 grades 11-12 subjects and 20 out of 22 of the adults divided the words appropriately.[4]

The poor performance of the younger groups might seem surprising in view of the fact that in their school, parts of speech are taught from the second grade on. Teachers informed the writer that their pupils have great difficulty with the concept of parts of speech. The notion of form class is taught in this school, as it is in most, in terms of semantic correlates. For example, a noun is defined by the text used by these students as a *person*, *place*, *thing*, or *idea*. The apparent difficulty met by students in grasping such concepts accords again with the generalization hypothesis. General concepts are difficult to appreciate at an early age.

Conclusions

The tendency for adults to sort words according to part of speech more often than children has been replicated. A decrease with age in the tendency to cluster words bound by relations which might be called thematic has also been noted. Figures 3.6-3.10 show that the difference between the behavior of adults and the behavior of children can be described in detail. Children cluster opposites as often as do adults. The difference between the extent of clustering for the two groups increases directly with the abstractness of the relations among words. These findings are consonant with the generalization hypothesis.

The empirical verification of the notion of degree of abstractness provided by the first sorting experiment has been replicated. The adults' sorting behavior in this experiment reflects the hierarchical organization of the words more than does the children's behavior. This is true for both group and individual data. Adults are more consistent among one another in their divisions and subdivisions of the words than children who are more idiosyncratic. The younger subjects appear not to understand the concept of parts of speech which had been taught in their English classes. Their apparent difficulty with this idea accords with the view that abstract notions are difficult to master in childhood.

[4] Inadvertently the writer failed to test two adults.

4 The Free Recall and Free Association Experiments

The Free Recall Study

The most commonly voiced criticism of the sorting technique concerns the ambiguity of the instructions. Such criticism has been directed toward the developmental results particularly often. The argument states that since psychologists, philosophers, and linguists cannot agree upon a definition of meaning, one should not expect the subjects to be able to do so either. In the case of the developmental results, the argument states that the phrase *similarity of meaning* is interpreted differently by the different age groups, that in fact the young subjects are baffled by the instructions, and that an explanation of differences between adults and children in terms of different underlying lexical structures is therefore not necessary.

The criticism is in some ways reminiscent of the argument directed at Stevens' first studies in magnitude estimation (Stevens 1957) in which it was asserted that subjects could not be assumed to understand the complexities of the number system well enough to generate ratios. Such criticisms of "direct methods" are deficient in that they focus only on the instructions without regard to the order which does in fact emerge upon analysis of the data. Neither Stevens' power functions nor our Figures 3.6-3.10 suggest a failure of understanding on the part of the subjects. The data are too systematic. In our case the uniformity with which the children deal with the opposites and certain other word-pairs denies that the instructions are meaningless even to them.

Nonetheless it was felt desirable to attempt to replicate the major findings of Chapter 1 by using a technique which involved different instructions, and, in particular, which did not involve use of the phrase *similarity of meaning*. For this purpose we have chosen the free recall task because of its formal similarity, outlined in Chapter 1, to the sorting task. The use of free recall is thus analogous to Stevens' use of cross-modality matching (e.g., J. C. Stevens and Marks 1965).

Method

There were four groups of subjects with ten males and ten females per group. The three youngest groups consisted of students from the grades 3-4, grades 7-8, and grades 11-12 classes of the Scarsdale public school system. According to the teachers over 90 percent of their students go to four-year colleges upon graduation. The fourth group, the adults, was made up of graduate students and research assistants at The Rockefeller University. The median ages for the groups were 9, 13, 16.5, and 23.5 years, respectively. Every subject was tested individually.

There were two parts to an experimental session.

Part 1: To begin with, a subject was asked to sit in a chair in front of a table on which there were two tape recorders. The subject was told that when the test was to start he would hear a list of twenty words on one of the tape recorders. He was to listen to them and as soon as the list had been completed the experimenter would give him a signal. When he heard the signal he was to recall as many of the twenty words as he could by speaking them loudly into a microphone that was connected to the other tape recorder. He was allowed to recall them in any order he wanted. The subject was told that this process would be repeated for ten trials.

The tape recorder had been preset so that the words would be clearly audible, but not uncomfortably loud. On each of the ten trials the words were presented in a different random order. The same random orders were used for all subjects. The subject was allowed as much time as he wanted for recall, although he was asked to try not to repeat any of the words within a given recall. This part of the experiment usually lasted from thirty to forty minutes.

Part 2: While the subject was recalling the words, the experimenter was writing them down in the order in which they occurred on a sheet of paper. At the end of the tenth trial the subject was handed the sheet of paper and a pencil and was asked to indicate which words he "remembered in groups" by inserting lines in his protocols. Lines were to reflect group boundaries. He was to start with the tenth trial and to proceed backwards until he had finished the first trial. This part of the experiment usually lasted about ten minutes.

Results and Discussion

A Close Look at Developmental Trends in Free Recall. The results have been analyzed in two ways corresponding to the two parts of the experiment. The first set of analyses has been applied to the original protocols and has ignored the lines drawn by the subjects; the second set has been applied to the clusters defined by those lines.

Set 1: The family of curves in Figure 4.1 shows that the average number of words correctly recalled increases with trials and with age. By the tenth trial the adults remember an average of about nineteen words while the grades 3-4 children remember an average of about fifteen. The other two age groups fall between the two extremes.

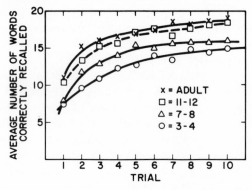

Figure 4.1. Average number of words correctly recalled in the free recall task as a function of trial number for the different age groups.

To estimate the extent of paradigmatic clustering (P.C.) the following statistic was calculated: $P.C. = \Sigma R / \max \Sigma R$. ΣR is the total number of paradigmatic repetitions within a protocol. Max ΣR represents the number of such repetitions that would occur in the same protocol if its members were rearranged so that words of a given part of speech were not separated by words of another part of speech. A paradigmatic repetition occurs every time two words of the same part of speech are adjacent in the protocol. This statistic was chosen because it is roughly independent of the number of words recalled.[1] In the computation both repetitions and intrusions have been included.

---

[1] On the assumption of random arrangement of a given protocol the expected value of this statistic is constant and equal to $1/p$ where p is the number of parts of speech *if* the same number of items per part of speech is recalled. Thus in this case the chance value under the assumption of a random arrangement of the words is equal to 0.25 given that a protocol contains an equal number of nouns, verbs, adjectives, and prepositions. Violations of this assumption inflate the expected value of the statistic slightly.

In Figure 4.2 we have compared the average value of this statistic for the different age groups for two sets of protocols. First we equated for exposure to the material and calculated the statistic for the tenth trial for all subjects. Figure 4.2 shows that the average value of this statistic rises with age. Second we equated for the number of words in a protocol. On the tenth trial there was an average of 16 words in the protocols of the grades 3-4 children. An average of 16 words appeared in the protocols of the grades 7-8, grades 11-12, and adult groups on the fifth, third, and second trials, respectively. The statistic was calculated and averaged for each of these. Figure 4.2 shows that the degree of paradigmatic clustering again rises with age when the number of words in recall is equated. Mann-Whitney U tests showed that these statistics were reliably greater for the adults than for the children ($Z = 3.05$, $p < 0.002$; $Z = 3.31$, $p < 0.001$).

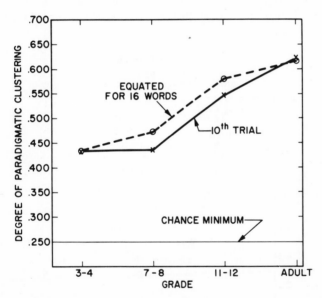

Figure 4.2. Degree of paradigmatic clustering for the different age groups in the free recall task.

In order to examine the fine structure of the increase in paradigmatic clustering with age the following analysis was performed. For each age group the total number of times two words were clustered on the tenth trial was calculated for every pair of words of the same part of speech. Cluster boundaries were defined by a change in part of speech in the protocols. This total was then divided by the total number of times the two words were both remembered by the same subject on the tenth trial.

Thus in order to be included in the calculation for a given word-pair a subject was required to have remembered both of the words in that pair.

Figures 4.3-4.7 show the results of this analysis and depict the major finding of this chapter. These graphs are directly analogous to Figures 3.6-3.10 in that the statistics described above have been averaged in the same way for the various word-pairs. For example, Figure 4.3 shows for the different age groups the average percentage of noun-pairs clustered as a function of the generality of the presumed minimal feature. Figures 4.4, 4.5, and 4.6 are similar graphs for the prepositions, verbs, and adjectives. Figure 4.7 represents this phenomenon averaged over parts of speech.

By and large, adult curves tend to be decreasing functions of the presumed minimal features, although only the curve for the prepositions is monotonic. In spite of the noise and in view of the average effect seen in Figure 4.7 to be monotonic, these graphs suggest that shared features may

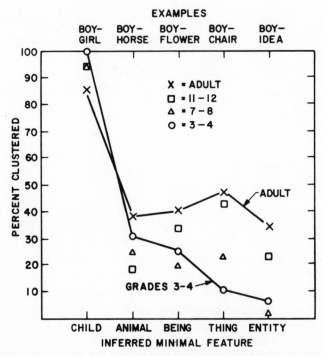

Figure 4.3. Extent of noun clustering in the free recall task as a function of the generality of the relation between nouns for the different age groups.

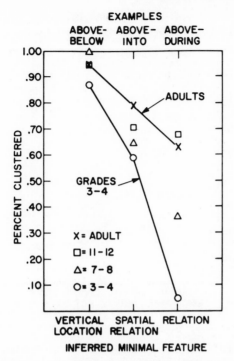

Figure 4.4. Extent of preposition clustering in the free recall task as a function of the generality of the relation between prepositions for the different age groups.

be important in the organization of free recall as they are in Miller's sorting task. Undoubtedly other factors are also operative.

Also, as in the second sorting experiment, the curves for the adults and the children tend to diverge as the generality of the relation between the words increases. In fact the difference between the extent of clustering for adults and for children grows monotonically in the case of the prepositions and the adjectives. One difference is out of line for the nouns and one for the verbs (surprisingly, the opposites). Points for the other age groups usually fall between the curves for adults and children.

The diverging curves of Figures 4.3-4.7 corroborate the sorting results in suggesting that children are able to make use of the concrete equivalence relations among words, but are not as likely as are adults to make use of more abstract relations. Thus, these data, like the sorting data, are consistent with the generalization hypothesis.

Part 2: The clusters produced by the subjects' lines on the tenth trial

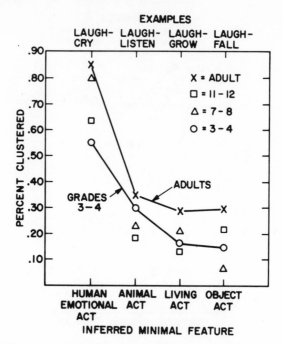

Figure 4.5. Extent of verb clustering in the free recall task as a function of the generality of the relation between verbs for the different age groups.

were used to construct incidence matrices which were then added. Omissions were treated as singletons. The resulting matrices were then subjected to Johnson's hierarchical clustering program. Figure 4.8 shows the results of the diameter method for adults. Three of the five trees are of the same part of speech. *Angry* has joined the emotion verbs *laugh* and *cry*, and *idea* has been combined with the other verbs *listen*, *fall*, and *grow*. The tendency to respect the part of speech classification was highly significant for adults ($Z = 5.66, p < 0.001$).

However, the hierarchical structure of Figure 1.1 has only partially emerged in Figure 4.8. There are only two clear manifestations of this hierarchical structure: (1) the opposites have been clustered more often than other word-pairs of the same part of speech, and (2) the tree for prepositions corresponds exactly to the theoretical tree in its ordinal relations. In general, though, the sorting task appears to be more sensitive to such class inclusion relations than the free recall task.

Figure 4.9 shows the trees for the children. Only two out of eight trees are of the same part of speech. The only words clustered with any con-

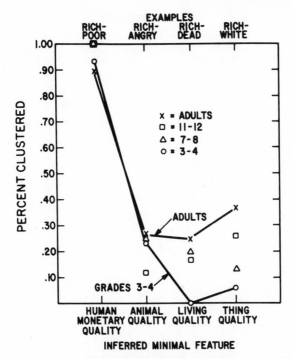

Figure 4.6. Extent of adjective clustering in the free recall task as a function of the generality of the relation between adjectives for the different age groups.

sistency are the opposites, and of these even the tendency to group *laugh* and *cry* is weak. This is partly due to the fact that subjects in this group remembered an average of only fifteen words on the last trial. It is also partly due to the fact that these subjects tended to leave most words as singles in their groupings. A Mann-Whitney U test showed that subjects in this group formed smaller clusters than the adults ($Z = 4.13$, $p < 0.001$). This largely accounts for the fact that the distances of the adults' clusterings from the part of speech clustering were significantly less than those of the children's clusterings ($Z = 3.19$, $p < 0.001$). A Mann-Whitney U test on the respect ratios for the two groups showed that children's clusters also tended to be more syntagmatic ($Z = 2.11$, $p < 0.02$) as well.

Individual Differences. Trees for individual subjects have also been computed by using each of a subject's ten trials to generate a matrix. A casual inspection of the results suggested that the trees of adults tended to be more idiosyncratic than comparable trees from the sorting task. Free recall

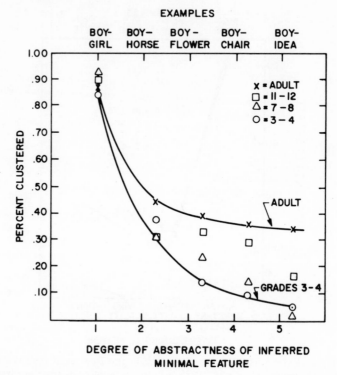

Figure 4.7. Extent of clustering as a function of the generality of the relation between words in the free recall study averaged over parts of speech.

trees for adults seemed somewhat more consistent than those for children. Figures 4.10 and 4.11 show the resulting trees for one adult and one child. D. F., the adult, was noticeably paradigmatic in his clusterings, as Figure 4.10 reveals. Figure 4.11 showing the trees for B. C., a child, contrasts with Figure 4.10 in that most trees are heterogeneous by part of speech.

To assess intersubject variability more objectively, similarity measures were computed using the tenth trial matrices for each of the 780 possible pairs of adults and children. This similarity measure was the same as that used in the analysis of the data from the original sorting experiment. These were subjected to the Kruskal-Shepard multidimensional scaling program. Figure 4.12 shows the two-dimensional solution which has a stress of 0.28. There appears to be a separation of the adults from the children. Moreover, whereas most adults coalesce in the first quadrant, the children are scattered throughout the other three. This suggests that adults are more

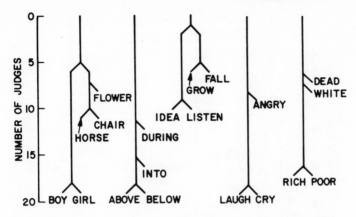

Figure 4.8. Free recall hierarchies for adults (diameter method).

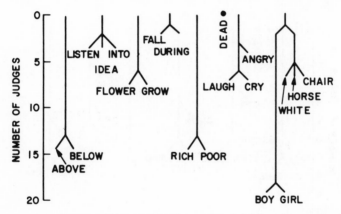

Figure 4.9. Free recall hierarchies for grades 3-4 (diameter method).

consistent in their response to the task than are children, at least on the tenth trial.

Conclusions

The free recall technique appears to be less sensitive to the hierarchical relations among words than is the sorting technique. Nonetheless the major findings of Chapter 3 have here been replicated with a task involving totally different instructions. Adults' clusters are more paradigmatic than those of children. Children's clusters are more syntagmatic, smaller, and more idiosyncratic than those of adults. Figures 4.3-4.7 suggest that shared features may serve as a basis in the organization of free recall for adults,

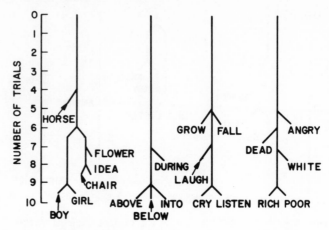

Figure 4.10. Free recall hierarchies for D. F., adult (diameter method).

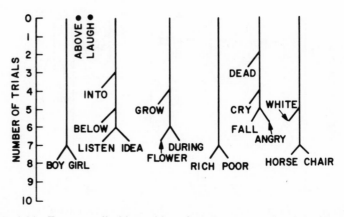

Figure 4.11. Free recall hierarchies for B. C., grade 3-4 (diameter method).

although other factors are probably operative as well. Moreover, the diverging curves of Figures 4.3-4.7 tend to support the generalization hypothesis.

The Free Association Task

Some free recall data can be predicted from free association data (Deese 1965, Jenkins and Russell 1952, Rothkopf and Coke 1961). Although a correlation between free recall and free association data does not consti-

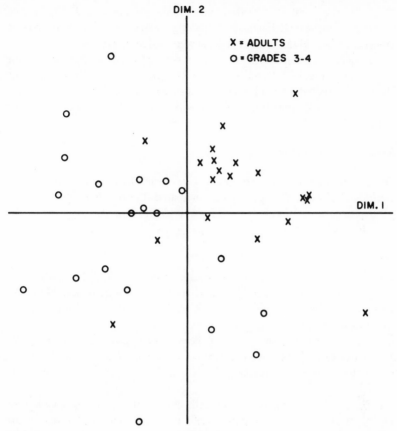

Figure 4.12. The two-dimensional subject space for the free recall study (Kruskal-Shepard).

tute an explanation of either (see Chapter 1), it was decided to collect some free association norms of our own in an attempt to see what similarities would be revealed by comparing these norms with the sorting and free recall results.

Method

There were four groups of subjects with 25 males and 25 females per group. The youngest groups consisted of students from the grades 3-4, grades 7-8, and grades 11-12 classes of the Dalton School in New York. According to Hechinger and Hechinger (1968), over 95 percent of its students go to four-year colleges upon graduation. The fourth group, the adults, were individuals in The Rockefeller University area who responded to an advertisement. The median ages for the groups were 9, 13, 17, and 22 years, respectively. Each of the three youngest age-levels was tested in groups; subjects in the oldest age-level were tested individually.

A subject was handed a sheet of paper with 24 words written on it – the 20 words of Figure 1.1 and four adverbs (*happily*, *sadly*, *loudly*, *truly*).[2] He was instructed to read each stimulus word and to write beside it the first word it made him think of. Subjects spent about ten minutes at the task.

Results and Discussion

Comparison of Free Association and Clustering Findings. The intersection coefficient (Deese 1965, p. 51) was calculated for every word-pair for each of the age groups. This coefficient is given by the formula:

$$IC = \frac{S_A \cap S_B}{\sqrt{N_A \cdot N_B}}$$

where the numerator represents the intersection of the distributions of responses for words A and B and where the denominator represents the geometric mean of the number of responses in each distribution. Every stimulus word is assumed by Deese to elicit itself as a response along with the written response, so that the denominator in our case is always 100. This measure of associative overlap increases when one of the two words elicits the other as a response and when the two words share a response in common.

Table 4.1 shows a matrix whose cells contain the associative overlap for adults for all possible word-pairs. Apart from the opposites the word-pairs have a minimally small associative overlap. Most cell entries have a value of 0 and none has a value greater than 8 percent except those for the opposites. Table 4.2 shows a similar matrix for the grades 3-4 children. Again apart from the cells for the opposites no entry has a value greater than 7 percent and most cells read 0. The matrices for the grades 7-8 and grades 11-12 groups were similar to Tables 4.1 and 4.2.

These results are not really surprising to us and they probably would not be to Deese. They sound very much like Deese's description of the matrix that would result from a random selection of words from the lexicon: "If we pick words at random from the dictionary and from these words prepare a matrix . . . , the result is a vast sea of zero entries, dotted here and

[2] Originally we had intended to use these adverbs in all studies. For various reasons we decided against the use of adverbs, but only after the free association forms had been printed. Responses to adverbs were ignored in the analyses.

Table 4.1. Matrix Showing Associative Overlap (after Deese 1965) of Word-Pairs for Adults ($N = 50$).

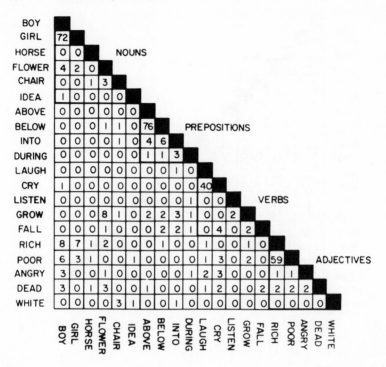

	BOY	GIRL	HORSE	FLOWER	CHAIR	IDEA	ABOVE	BELOW	INTO	DURING	LAUGH	CRY	LISTEN	GROW	FALL	RICH	POOR	ANGRY	DEAD
BOY																			
GIRL	72																		
HORSE	0	0																	
FLOWER	4	2	0																
CHAIR	0	0	1	3															
IDEA	1	0	0	0	0														
ABOVE	0	0	0	0	0	0													
BELOW	0	0	0	1	1	0	76												
INTO	0	0	0	0	1	0	4	6											
DURING	0	0	0	0	0	0	1	1	3										
LAUGH	0	0	0	0	0	0	0	0	0	1									
CRY	1	0	0	0	0	0	0	0	0	0	40								
LISTEN	0	0	0	0	0	0	0	0	0	0	1	0							
GROW	0	0	0	8	1	0	2	2	3	1	0	0	2						
FALL	0	0	0	1	0	0	0	2	2	1	0	4	0	2					
RICH	8	7	1	2	0	0	0	1	0	0	1	0	0	1	0				
POOR	6	3	1	0	0	1	0	0	0	0	1	3	0	2	0	59			
ANGRY	3	0	0	1	0	0	0	0	0	1	2	3	0	0	0	1	1		
DEAD	3	0	1	3	0	0	1	0	0	0	1	2	0	0	2	2	2	2	
WHITE	0	0	0	3	1	0	0	1	0	0	0	0	0	0	0	0	0	0	0

Group labels in the upper region: NOUNS, PREPOSITIONS, VERBS, ADJECTIVES.

there by some positive values usually low in magnitude" (Deese 1965, p. 57). The twenty words of this study have been taken from diverse sections of the lexicon and hence such a result may well have been anticipated. However, Deese's statement that "organized tables of associative meaning may be achieved by almost any method that takes advantage of the relations among concepts and words in a language" (p. 57) is in the light of Tables 5 and 6 an overgeneralization.

The traditional free association test does not appear to be sensitive to the kinds of relations which are tapped by the sorting and free recall techniques. It is true that the opposites which have high associative overlap are the words which are clustered most often in these tasks. In this respect there is a correlation. However, neither the extent of clustering nor the differences among the age groups in these tasks can be predicted from measures of associative overlap for other word-pairs. To make this point, in Figure 4.13 we have plotted the associative overlap averaged over parts of speech for each age group as a function of the generality of the relation

Table 4.2. Matrix Showing Associative Overlap (after Deese 1965) of Word-Pairs for Grades 3-4 ($N = 50$).

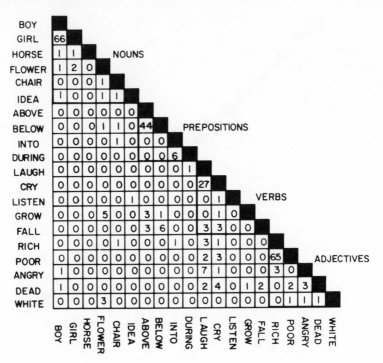

	BOY	GIRL	HORSE	FLOWER	CHAIR	IDEA	ABOVE	BELOW	INTO	DURING	LAUGH	CRY	LISTEN	GROW	FALL	RICH	POOR	ANGRY	DEAD	WHITE
BOY																				
GIRL	66																			
HORSE	1	1				NOUNS														
FLOWER	1	2	0																	
CHAIR	0	0	0	1																
IDEA	1	0	0	1	1															
ABOVE	0	0	0	0	0	0														
BELOW	0	0	0	1	1	0	44			PREPOSITIONS										
INTO	0	0	0	0	1	0	0	0												
DURING	0	0	0	0	0	0	0	0	6											
LAUGH	0	0	0	0	0	0	0	0	0	1										
CRY	0	0	0	0	0	0	0	0	0	0	27									
LISTEN	0	0	0	0	0	1	0	0	0	0	0	1	VERBS							
GROW	0	0	0	5	0	0	3	1	0	0	0	1	0							
FALL	0	0	0	0	0	0	3	6	0	0	3	3	0	0						
RICH	0	0	0	0	1	0	0	0	1	0	3	1	0	0	0					
POOR	0	0	0	0	0	0	0	0	0	0	2	3	0	0	0	65	ADJECTIVES			
ANGRY	1	0	0	0	0	0	0	0	0	0	7	1	0	0	0	3	0			
DEAD	1	0	0	0	0	0	0	0	0	0	2	4	0	1	2	0	2	3		
WHITE	0	0	0	3	0	0	0	0	0	0	0	0	0	0	0	0	0	1	1	1

between word-pairs. The points in Figure 4.13 have been computed as were the points in Figures 3.10 and 4.7, but the results are clearly different. In Figure 4.13 the associative overlap for words other than opposites is minimal and does not reflect the extent of clustering of these words in sorting and free recall. Moreover, the relation between associative overlap and degree of generality can be represented by the same curve for all age groups.

We have examined the data in another way in an attempt to find a correlation between the free association results and the sorting and free recall results. Figure 4.14 shows the average proportion of responses that are homogeneous by part of speech for the different ages. There is more of a difference among the parts of speech than among the age groups. A Mann-Whitney U test did show that adults are significantly more paradigmatic in their responses than children ($Z = 2.59$, $p < 0.01$). But the difference was small—less than an average of two out of twenty words. Moreover, as Figure 4.14 shows, the grades 7-8 group and the grades 11-12 group actually produced more paradigmatic responses than did adults.

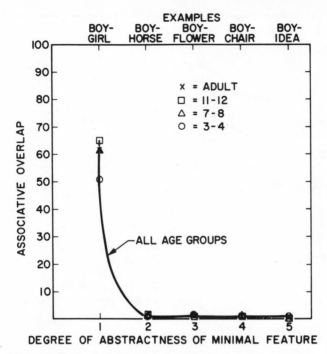

Figure 4.13. Associative overlap as a function of the generality of the relation between words averaged over parts of speech.

Why No Age-Related Differences in Free Association? The free association data are actually consistent with the generalization theory of lexical growth given the assumption that an associate is very closely related to its stimulus. An inspection of the data suggest that this assumption may be valid, although we have no criteria for assessing proximity. The most common responses of the grades 3-4 children for one member of a pair of opposites was the other member of the pair. Thus these responses were concrete associates in the sense of Chapter 1. Associates to other words bore what might be called a concrete relation to their stimuli as well. The most common paradigmatic responses to the other words were as follows: *pony* to *horse*, *rose* to *flower*, *table* to *chair*, *out of* to *into*, *after* to *during*, *hear* to *listen*, *shrink* to *grow*, *hurt* to *fall*, *mad* to *angry*, *alive* to *dead*, and *black* to *white*. Many of these word-pairs comprise bipolar contrasts (Deese 1962, 1964). The rest, with the possible exception of the response *hurt* to *fall*, which seem to be related thematically, might be described by Katz as sharing many semantic markers and might well be clustered together by many adults in Miller's sorting task. In short, chil-

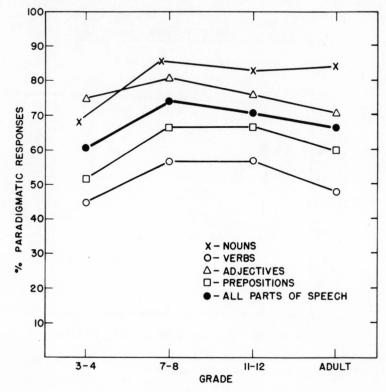

Figure 4.14. Percent of paradigmatic associates for the different age groups.

dren's responses in the free association task appear to be related to the stimuli in a way that we have been describing as concrete.

If this is so then the flat curves of Figure 4.14 should not surprise us. The sorting and free recall data have already suggested that words bound by concrete relations are dealt with in the same way by both adults and children. The free association task appears to tap only concrete relations and hence no large differences among these age groups emerge.

Conclusions

Different tasks used in the experimental analysis of meaning are sensitive to different things. There is a correlation between the associative overlap for opposites and the extent of clustering these words in the other experiments. However, neither the extent of clustering nor the differences among age groups can be predicted from association norms for other word-pairs, at least not from those collected and analyzed in the usual way. Whether some alternative form of generating free association results (e.g., "constrained association") would yield data that would correlate with our major findings is an open question. Although no large differences with age were observed, the free association data appear to be compatible with the generalization theory of lexical growth.

5 What the Clustering Studies Mean

The results from the clustering studies (sorting and free recall) have provided the primary empirical phenomena of this book. These results can neither be explained by nor predicted from free association norms collected and analyzed in the usual way. The purpose of the experiments described in this chapter was to cast some light on what the clustering findings do and do not mean.

The Frames Experiment

When a child in grades 3 or 4 is asked to sort the twenty words into piles on the basis of similarity of meaning, when he is asked to sort them according to form class, or when he is asked to recall them in any order he wants, he consistently ignores the part of speech distinction that so often seems important to an adult. The following simple experiment was contrived to see if we could lure a child into respecting the distinction. We were also curious to see whether children of this age really can speak the language, or more specifically whether they can put words into their proper places in sentences. In view of Brown's (1957) observations we expected they could.

Method

The subjects consisted of five boys and five girls from the Murray Hill area in New Jersey. Three subjects had just finished grade 1; two, grade 2; three, grade 3; one, grade 4; and one, grade 5. The median age was eight years.

72

In an experimental session a subject was seated in front of a table on which there were a sheet of paper and an envelope. The sheet was divided into four quadrants in each of which appeared a sentence frame. The sentence frames were as follows: For the nouns, "The ___ is good"; for the verbs, "The people ___ "; for the adjectives, "The ___ man is here"; and for the prepositions, "They fly ___ the storm." The idea of using such frames was borrowed from Fries (1952).

The subject was told that the experimenter was going to take a word out of the envelope and place it into each of the sentence frames. He would be required to read each frame including the word as it was placed into its slot. After the subject had read the four frames he was to be asked which of the frames was a real sentence. He would be allowed to choose only one. This process was to be repeated for all of the twenty words.

The words had been shuffled in the envelope prior to an experimental session. Each word was accompanied by a sense specifying definition as in the sorting experiments. The order of sentence frames was the same for all words and for all subjects. The order was noun frame, verb frame, adjective frame, and preposition frame. The task usually lasted about ten minutes per subject.

Results

All subjects could read the frames and the words. Seven out of ten subjects respected completely the distinction based on parts of speech. They put the words into the proper form class frames. The remaining three subjects violated the form class distinction once each. Two of them put *flower* in the frame "The ___ man is here." The result would probably be considered an English sentence to most adults. One subject put *dead* in the frame "The ___ is good."

Conclusions

Children can put these twenty words into their proper places in simple English sentence frames. When provided with such frames they can sort the words into the four parts of speech. The clustering results do not mean that children cannot use the words properly in sentences.

The Bower Experiment

The ability to put two words into the same sentence frame does not necessarily imply an ability to see a relation between those words in the absence of sentence frames. To gauge the capacity of individuals of different ages to extract and make use of the relations that exist among the twenty words we have borrowed a technique from Bower et al. (1969)

(with minor modifications) because of its apparent sensitivity to intra-verbal relations. This sensitivity was described in Chapter 1.

Method

There were 4 groups of subjects with 12 males and 24 females in each. The youngest groups consisted of students from the grades 3-4, grades 7-8, and grades 11-12 classes of St. Hilda's and St. Hugh's, a private school in New York. According to Hechinger and Hechinger (1968) about 98 percent of its students go to four-year colleges upon graduation. The fourth group, the adults, consisted of graduate and undergraduate students at New York University and also one faculty member. The median ages for the groups were 9, 13, 17, and 21 years, respectively. All age-levels were tested in groups.

Within each age group, subjects were haphazardly divided into 4 sub-groups with 3 males and 6 females per subgroup. Each subject was handed a booklet containing 5 pages. The subjects were told that soon they would be given a signal upon which they were to turn to the third page of the booklet, on which they would see four tree-like diagrams with words at the ends of the branches of the trees. A tree diagram was then drawn on the blackboard to demonstrate what was meant. The subjects' task was to memorize as many of the words on the page as they could. Specifically they were to try to remember exactly where on the diagram the words appeared, and which words appeared next to one another. For when the study period was over they were to be presented with another page with the same tree diagrams on it, but in this case the words would appear at the bottom of the page. Their task would be to write the words in the exact place where they had occurred on the study sheet. They were to have exactly 90 seconds to study and as long as they wished to write their responses on the test sheet.

On each study sheet four trees were arranged vertically so that the top tree had six branches, the second tree had five branches, the third tree had five branches, and the bottom tree had four branches. There were four types of study sheets, one for each of the subgroups. On two the material was structured (ST_1, ST_2); on two it was scrambled (SC_1, SC_2). On ST_1 sheets the trees were right branching. Nouns were placed at the ends of the branches of the top tree as they are in Figure 1.1. From left to right they read *boy, girl, horse, flower, chair, idea*. The verbs, adjectives, and preposi-tions were placed at the ends of the branches of the second, third, and fourth trees, respectively. The order of placement was also the same as in Figure 1.1 for these parts of speech. An ST_1 study sheet is shown in Figure 5.1.

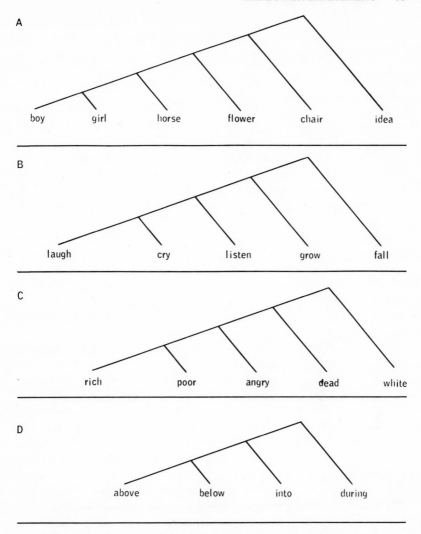

Figure 5.1. An ST_1 study sheet used in the Bower experiment.

On ST_2 sheets the trees were left branching. Again nouns were placed at the ends of branches of the top tree. The order of placement of words on ST_2 sheets was exactly the reverse of that for ST_1 sheets. For example, from *right to left* the order for nouns was *boy*, *girl*, *horse*, *flower*, *chair*, *idea*. The verbs, adjectives, and prepositions were placed at the ends of the branches of the second, third, and fourth trees similarly. An ST_2 sheet is shown in Figure 5.2.

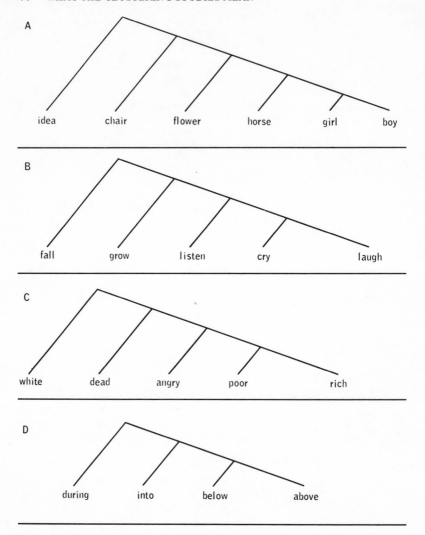

Figure 5.2. An ST_2 study sheet used in the Bower experiment.

The scrambled study sheets showed the same trees and the same words as the structured ones but the words had been placed in a random order at the ends of the branches. The trees of SC_1 were right branching; the same random order was used on all SC_1 sheets. The trees of SC_2 sheets were left branching; the order of the words for each tree in an SC_2 sheet was exactly the reverse of the order on an SC_1 sheet for the corresponding tree. The scrambled study sheets are shown in Figures 5.3 and 5.4.

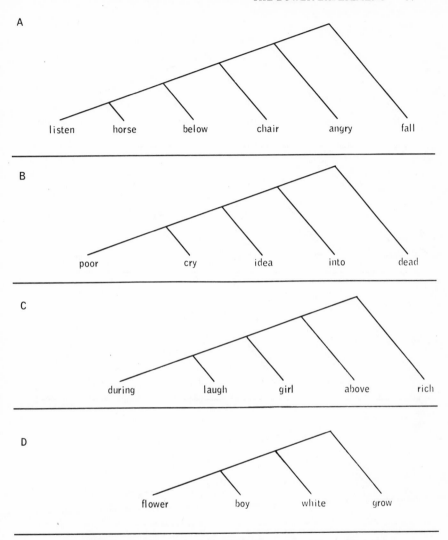

Figure 5.3. An SC_1 study sheet used in the Bower experiment.

After the experimenter had gone over the procedure in detail and after all questions had been answered, the study session began. The study interval was timed with a stopwatch. As soon as 90 seconds had elapsed, subjects were instructed to close their booklets immediately. Then they were asked to turn them over. On the back of the fifth page of each booklet appeared a test sheet on which there were trees arranged as the trees of the

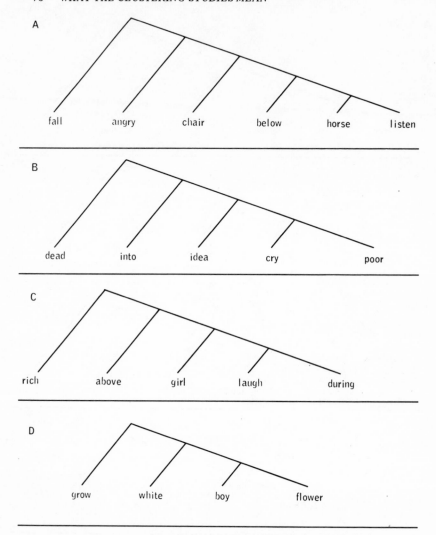

Figure 5.4. An SC_2 study sheet used in the Bower experiment.

study sheet. The words were not at the ends of the branches, however, but rather appeared at the bottom of the page randomly arranged in four columns. The same random arrangement of columns was used for all subjects. A test sheet is shown in Figure 5.5.

It was the impression of the experimenter that sessions ran smoothly. Subjects had no trouble finding the third page of the booklet, the study

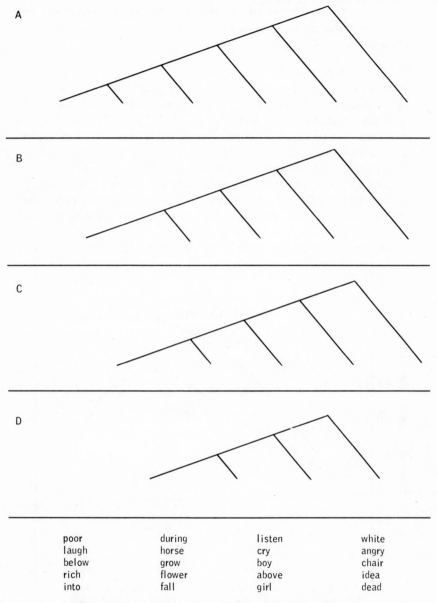

poor	during	listen	white
laugh	horse	cry	angry
below	grow	boy	chair
rich	flower	above	idea
into	fall	girl	dead

Figure 5.5. A test sheet used in the Bower experiment.

atmosphere was quiet, and subjects closed their booklets as soon as they were told. Subjects typically spent from 10 to 15 minutes writing the words on the test sheet.

Results and Discussion

The total number of words correctly placed at the ends of the branches was calculated for every subject. An analysis of variance revealed that there was a significant age effect ($F_{3,128} = 19.70, p < 0.01$), a significant structure effect ($F_{1,128} = 24.26, p < 0.01$), and a significant structure by age interaction ($F_{3,128} = 4.72, p < 0.01$). Figure 5.6 makes these effects clear. In Figure 5.6 we have averaged over the two orders of presentation for each age group and thus each point is the mean for eighteen subjects. The age effect is reflected in Figure 5.6 by the fact that the two curves rise with age. The point for the adults that deviates in the 'scrambled' curve

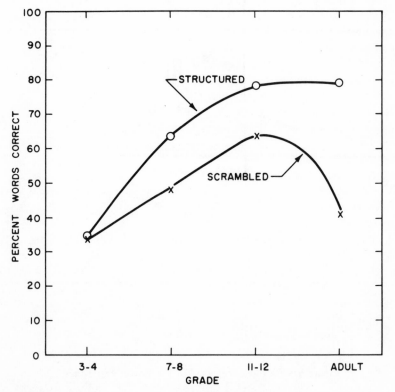

Figure 5.6. Percent words correct following structured and scrambled presentation for the different age groups.

will be considered below. With the exception of this point the percentage of words correctly placed on the test sheet increases with age. The structure effect shows up in the separation of the two curves. More words were correctly placed on the test sheet when the study sheet was structured than when it was scrambled. The structure by age interaction reveals itself in the divergence of the two curves. The grades 3-4 children benefit little if at all from the structured material relative to the scrambled material, whereas adults perform about twice as well with the organized study sheet. The facilitation derived from the organized material can be seen to be intermediate between these two extremes for the middle age groups.

The analysis of variance also showed a significant order effect $(F_{1,128} = 12.02, p < 0.01)$. Right-branching trees produced more facilitation than left-branching trees. This effect was stronger for the older groups than for the grades 3-4 children $(F = 5.48, df = 3,138, p < 0.01)$.

The most puzzling aspect of Figure 5.6 is that while the adults do better than the other age levels with structured material, they do not do as well as either the grades 11-12 or the grades 7-8 groups with the scrambled material. The overall quadratic effect for age is significant $(F = 22.78, df = 1,128, p < 0.01)$. In the light of Figure 5.6 most of this effect is accounted for by the inferior performance of adults on the scrambled material. We have no explanation for this inferiority. Perhaps some of the adults approached the task looking for a principle that would help them remember the material. If this were the case then their poor performance on the scrambled material might reflect time wasted in such a search that should have been spent in rote memorization. This interpretation is entirely conjectural, however.

The primary message of Figure 5.6 for our purposes is that adults appear to be able to make good use of the relations among the twenty words, whereas the grades 3-4 children appear less able to do so, if at all. Tallies of the number of words correctly placed is not the only way to measure the appreciation of structure, and probably not the most direct. For every pair of words that appeared side by side on the study sheet we have looked to see whether they appeared adjacent on the test sheet as well, regardless of whether they had been correctly placed. Figure 5.7 shows the percent of such adjacent word-pairs as a function of age level. All of the relations in Figure 5.6 appear to have been preserved when this measure of appreciation of structure is employed. There is a small separation of the two points for the grades 3-4 children. This separation was due to the opposites. In Figure 5.8 we have performed the same analysis as for Figure 5.7 except that we have left out the opposites and the word-pairs that corresponded to them on the 'scrambled' study sheets.

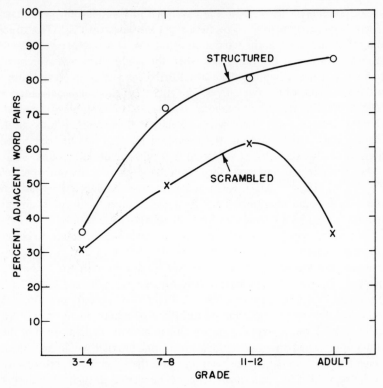

Figure 5.7. Percent adjacent word-pairs following structured and scrambled presentation for the different age groups.

When viewed in relation to the associative norms described in Chapter 4, Figure 5.8 suggests that the facilitation of the grades 3-4 children in this task can be predicted from the associative overlap of word-pairs, but the facilitation of the other age groups cannot. Our hypothesis is that the separation of the curves for the older age groups reflects an ability on the part of an active subject to extract and make use of the relations among words when they are presented in a display that conforms to those relations.

Conclusions

When adults are presented material that is organized spatially to conform to the categorical and hierarchical relations among words, the recall of adults reflects an apparent appreciation of those relations. The performance of children reflects such appreciation less. The relations to which

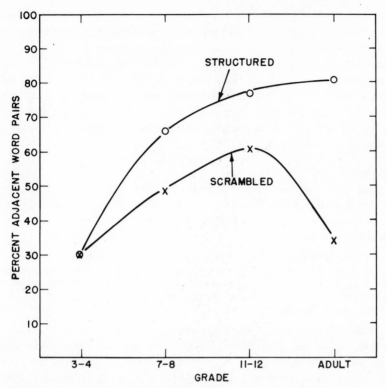

Figure 5.8. Percent adjacent word-pairs (excluding opposites) following structured and scrambled presentation for the different age groups.

adults seem sensitive might be described in terms of shared features. The developmental changes in the clustering studies may well reflect the same underlying phenomena as the developmental changes observed here. Specifically, they might both reflect an increase with age in the appreciation and use of the relations that make words equivalent.

The Bruner-Olver Experiment

If an adult's clusters reflect abilities to appreciate and to use the equivalence relations that bind words, perhaps he will be able to express those relations in the language. Suppose the diverging curves of Figures 3.6-3.10 and Figures 4.3-4.7 reflect different levels of appreciation by the different age groups. Then, perhaps, these different levels will show up in comparable differences in the capacity to describe equivalence relations among words. As we noted in Chapter 2, an inability to verbalize a concept does not necessarily imply a lack of appreciation of that concept. But verbal description presumably does set a lower bound on an individual's grasp of concepts. We have borrowed from the ideas of Bruner and Olver (1963, and Greenfield 1966) in an attempt to tap the extent to which subjects of different ages can describe the relations among words. There are many differences between our method and theirs. The most important of these is that the subject is required to state the equivalence relations only for word-pairs and not for larger groups of words. The reasons for this were outlined in Chapter 2.

Method

This study was conducted immediately after the material from the Bower experiment had been collected. The same subjects served. Subjects were handed another booklet, this one consisting of three pages. On the first page was a set of instructions which was read to the subjects:

On the next two pages there are forty-one pairs of words. Your task is to write above each pair what both words share in common, what makes them similar in meaning. For example, 'golf' and 'tennis' are both 'sports.' Do not write 'nouns' or 'verbs' or 'adjectives' or 'prepositions' above any of the pairs of words.

Then they were shown four more examples. These were *green* and *red*: *colors*; *before* and *after*: *times*; *diamond* and *ruby*: *precious stones*; and *kiss* and *hug*: *affectionate acts*. They were then told that they were not limited to one-word responses. They were to try to finish in thirty minutes. If they could not think of an answer for a particular word-pair they were to move on to the next. (In fact, if a subject did not feel that he had finished after thirty minutes he was given extra time.)

The 41 word-pairs were taken from the set of 20 words. They included the 15 possible pairs of nouns, the 10 possible pairs of verbs, the 10 possible pairs of adjectives, and the 6 possible pairs of prepositions. These word-pairs had been distributed randomly on the last two pages of each booklet. The random order was the same for every subject.

If a subject had a question he was to raise his hand and the experimenter went to talk to him privately. When subjects did have questions no information was given about how an individual word-pair should be handled; usually the experimenter dealt with questions by going over the instructions that had already been given. Most subjects worked quietly and finished before thirty minutes had elapsed.

Results and Discussion

The process of going over the resulting data has been a model of ad hoc analysis. The data have been analyzed three different times by two different individuals with each analysis involving a considerable relaxation of the criteria determining what would be accepted as a 'true similarity.' In some ways the reasons for the changes in analysis are as instructive as the final analysis itself. These will be described below. But first, one analysis of the data that was based upon an entirely objective measure will be presented.

The Objective Measure. Subjects either wrote something for a word-pair or they did not. The average number of written responses rose monotonically with age. A detailed analysis of the written responses is shown in Figure 5.9. The points in this graph have been computed as were the points of Figures 3.10 and 4.7. Figure 5.9 shows the average percentage of written responses for the different age groups as a function of the generality of the

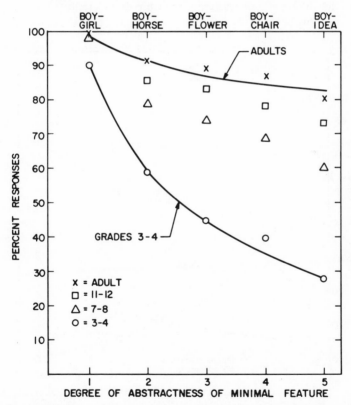

Figure 5.9. Percent responses as a function of the generality of the relation between words averaged over parts of speech.

relation between pairs of words averaged over parts of speech. Both the curve for the adults and the curve for the children are monotonically decreasing. Moreover, the difference between the proportion of responses for the two groups is monotonically increasing with the generality of the presumed relation.

In spite of the correspondence between Figure 5.9 and Figures 3.10 and 4.7 there is a reason that such an analysis fails to illuminate the clustering results entirely. Not all written responses were necessarily appropriate. Some were what we have since called *false superordinates* (e.g., *above* and *during: places*) and suggested that the subject did not see a relation between the two words even though he had written a response. Other responses seemed to involve putting the two words into a sentence (*boy, idea: Aristotle Onassis*). It is likely that any pair of the twenty words could be tied together with a third word in some sentence by most subjects, and differences in clustering probably do not reflect differences in such an ability. The curves of Figure 5.9 are higher than the corresponding

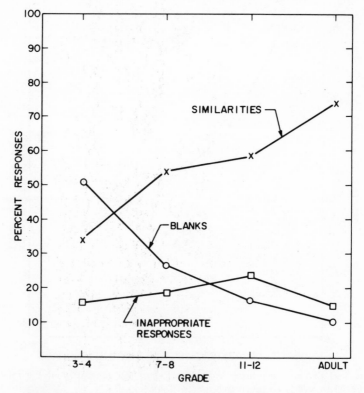

Figure 5.10. Patterns of responses for the different age groups.

curves of Figures 3.10 and 4.7 and this difference may well reflect an inflation due to inappropriate responses.

The Search for Criteria of Similarity of Meaning. With this we leave the realm of objectivity. For the above-mentioned reasons we have tried to devise a scoring system that would separate responses that were 'true similarities' from those that reflected failure to appreciate an equivalence relation. Three approaches were attempted, all of which made use of sentence frames.

In the first approach we used the frame "(All) _____ is (are) kind(s) of _____ ." If in our judgment the two stimulus words could meaningfully be fit into the first position of this frame when the response was put into the second position then that response was counted as a 'true similarity.'

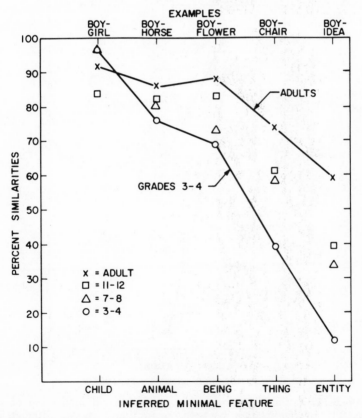

Figure 5.11. Percent similarities for nouns as a function of the generality of the relation between nouns for the different age groups.

Verbs, adjectives, and pronouns were nominalized. That is, for the purposes of the analysis we treated *laugh* as *laughing*, *rich* as *richness*, and *above* as *the state of being above*. At this time we were looking for the features of Figure 1.1 or their equivalents. This analysis, however, accounted for only about 25 percent of adult responses and for even less in the other age groups. Then we tried to relax our criterion somewhat by using the frame "(Some) _____ is (are) kind(s) of _____ ." so that the response did not have to be an appropriate predicate of the stimuli all of the time, but only some of the time. Partway through this analysis it became clear that again we were not accounting for the majority of the data and that we were missing responses that were describing genuine similarities among words. This led to the final analysis.

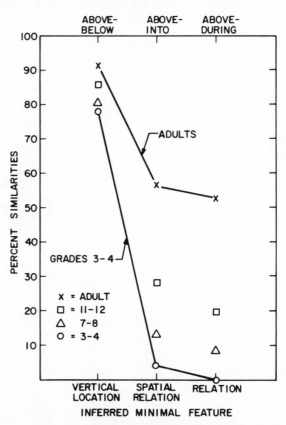

Figure 5.12. Percent similarities for prepositions as a function of the generality of the relation between prepositions for the different age groups.

In the final system the criterion for a response to be counted as a similarity was that that response had to bear the same relation to the two stimuli. That is, if the response in our judgment could be predicated of both stimuli then it was counted as a similarity. Moreover, it was not necessary that the response could be predicated of each stimulus all of the time but only some of the time. We continued to use sentence frames, but rather than one, we used about 14 which suggested themselves in the data. Table 5.1 shows the 8 frames most commonly used in this analysis with one example of its application for adults and one for children. The diversity of responses produced by subjects is only hinted at by Table 5.1. Nonetheless these examples make it clear that subjects were not con-

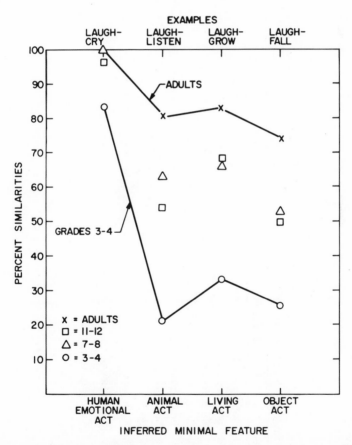

Figure 5.13. Percent similarities for verbs as a function of the generality of the relation between verbs for the different age groups.

Table 5.1 Sentence Frames and Examples.

Sentence Frame	Example: Adult	Example: Grades 3–4
1. Both _____ .	boy, flower: are alive	horse, boy: eat
2. Both are kinds of _____ .	rich, white: qualities	above, below: places
3. Both describe _____ .	rich, angry: upset executive	angry, white: people
4. Both are performed by _____ .	grow, fall: trees	cry, listen: you do both
5. Both imply _____ .	cry, listen: personal involvement	angry, dead: not nice
6. Both produce _____ .	girl, idea: inspiration	laugh, cry: noise
7. Both are signs of _____ .	laugh, cry: emotions	laugh, cry: moods
8. Both have _____ .	boy, flower: life cycle	boy, chair: legs
Thematic	boy, idea: Aristotle Onassis	boy, chair: sit
False Superordinate	above, during: places	rich, white: color

strained by our preconceptions concerning the relations among words. Figure 1.1 presents only a skeleton of the features shared by these words. Some of the examples in Table 5.1 do look like the nested features of Figure 1.1 or their equivalents. Such examples are *boy, flower: all alive*; *above, below: places*; *rich, white: qualities*; *laugh, cry: emotions*. But many others can be described as relations that are derivative from such nested features, or what Collins and Quillian (1969) call property relations. For example, the fact that *horse* and *boy* both *eat* is true by virtue of the fact that they both are *animals*; the fact that *boy* and *flower* both have *life cycles* is true by virtue of the fact that they both are *beings*. Some of the responses represent relations that were simply not

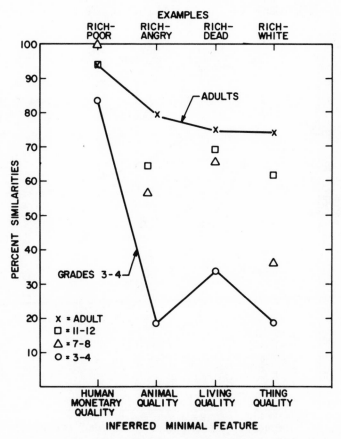

Figure 5.14. Percent similarities for adjectives as a function of the generality of the relation between adjectives for the different age groups.

anticipated. Examples of these are an evaluative response *not nice* to *angry* and *dead* or the simple relation of having *legs* that is usually true of both *boys* and *chairs*.

Table 5.1 shows examples of the two most common types of what we considered to be inappropriate responses. One of these was the thematic response. A response was counted as *thematic* when it seemed simply to be a possible sentence-mate of the two stimulus words and when it did not bear the same relation to them. An example here was *boy, chair: sit*. The other is the *false superordinate*. A response was counted as false super-ordinate when it seemed to be a genuine superordinate to one of the words but not to the other. An example of this was *rich, white: color*.

We are fully aware of the subjectivity involved in the analysis of these data. It is improbable that others would agree on certain classifications. In

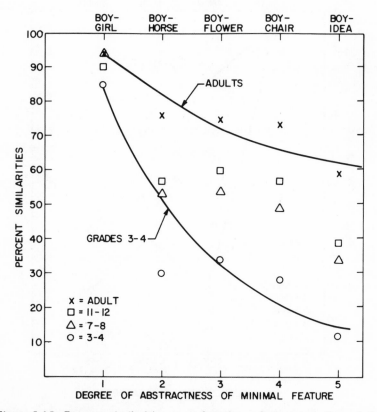

Figure 5.15. Percent similarities as a function of the generality of the relation between words averaged over parts of speech.

fact the two scorers disagreed more than once. We have, however, tried to be consistent in our classifications for all subjects in all age groups.

Comparison with Sorting and Free Recall. The overall pattern of the different types of responses for the different age groups is shown in Figure 5.10. The percentage of similarities increases with age, the percentage of blanks decreases with age, while the percentage of inappropriate responses remains fairly low and roughly constant. A Mann-Whitney U test showed that adults produced more similarities than the grades 3-4 children ($Z = 6.44, p \ll 0.001$).

A more detailed analysis of the distribution of similarities is shown in Figures 5.11-5.15. Once again we have depicted how groups perform with the generality of the relation between words. The curves of Figures 5.11-5.15 have the important characteristics of the corresponding curves for sorting and free recall: the adult curves are decreasing and the curves for children tend to diverge from the curves for adults. The correspondence among the three sets of curves is consistent with the notion that the sorting and free recall findings are, in part, a reflection of the ability on the part of subjects to actively generate a predicate that applies to the two members of a word-pair.

Conclusions

Many equivalence relations among the twenty words have not been depicted in Figure 1.1. When subjects are asked to verbalize what is similar about a word-pair they generate a host of relations. These can be viewed as predicates that can be applied to both members of a pair. An adult's ability to produce such predicates decreases with what we have called the generality of the relations among words. A child does almost as well as an adult at generating predicates for words bound by a concrete relation; a child does not do nearly so well as an adult when the relation is abstract. Clustering studies may, in part, be tapping the ability to generate such predicates.

6 Word Meaning and Semantic Development

In view of the data just reported, what can be said of the validity of the preconceptions underlying this work, of the appropriateness of their manifestations, and above all, of the light cast by these on the developmental question? How helpful has it been to view semantics in terms of features, to view features as hierarchically organized, to view sentences as the source of verbal concepts, and to view meaning as a social phenomenon? How appropriate are different clustering and association techniques in the experimental analysis of meaning and how valid is our belabored notion of abstractness? Finally, what can be said of the accretion of features, of the growth of the subjective lexicon and of the developing appreciation of language as a system? Some answers will be suggested in this chapter.

The Biases

The notion of a feature, as it was originally conceived, has taken a beating. In retrospect it required considerable innocence to attempt to specify the features that made the twenty words equivalent in terms of a single set of category labels. The last experiment described in this book has shown that subjects of all ages are not restricted by the few relations of Figure 1.1. Adult subjects appear to be able to generate a myriad of equivalence relations which for them make two words similar. A *boy* and a *horse* may both be *animals*, *beings*, *objects*, and *entities*, but they also both *eat*, *walk*, and *run*, they both have *legs*, *heads*, and *hair*, they both are *warm-blooded*, *active*, and *social*.

94

In fact, any time two words can be meaningfully followed by the same predicate they are equivalent along a dimension. Any time they can both serve as the subject of a higher-order language proposition (Russell 1940), they share meaning. This of course is no reflection on the analysis of proximities whether these are defined by piles, clusters, or associative heaps. It merely questions the validity of the inferential leap from pile to feature, from cluster to superordinate, or from heap to dimension. A subject's adherence to the structure built into an array of words is no assurance that he characterizes that structure in the way that the experimenter does. Most word-pairs within a part of speech can share several privileges of occurrence in the language many of which can be viewed as rendering them similar. The psychologist's predisposition to think in terms of "is a kind of" frames may not be met with a similar predisposition on the part of the subject. 'Has a,' 'describes a,' and 'is performed by a' are only a few of the many alternative possibilities.

Nonetheless there must be something to the notion of nested features as depicted in Figure 1.1. Twenty-five percent of adult subjects did generate such features when asked for the equivalence relations among words. More important, the adult data, particularly in the clustering experiments, conformed to the intuitions in accordance with which the words were chosen. These intuitions primarily concerned the features presumed to be shared by words. By and large adults were fairly uniform, particularly relative to children, in their sortings and clusters. This uniformity was manifest in the predicted ways. The hierarchical structure that had been built into the material was often retrieved. Opposites had the highest proximities in all tasks. Gross semantic distinctions most often conformed to the four parts of speech. Between the extremes, experimentally defined proximities changed predictably with intuitively defined shared features.

In view of the order in the data, the notion of presumed features should probably not be rejected entirely. If it is emphasized that the set of nested features of Figure 1.1 constitutes only a frame upon which a host of derivative or 'property' (Collins and Quillian 1969) relations can be hung, then the theoretical tree provides a useful heuristic.

There is something basic about the class-inclusion or "is a kind of" relation that is stressed so much by psychologists. Many of the other relations that make words equivalent are dependent on nested categories. Boys and horses *eat*, *walk*, and *run*, have *legs*, *heads*, and *hair*, are *warm-blooded*, *active*, and *social*, by virtue of the fact that they are both animals. If they were not animals, the above-mentioned predicates would not likely apply. A feature is a complex verbal concept rich in properties just as a word is. If the complexity and richness are acknowledged, an inferred set of nested features can serve as an abstraction useful in the prediction and understanding of the kinds of data that have been reported in this book.

The Tasks

Different techniques used in the experimental analysis of meaning appear at first glance to be tapping different things. A problem arises when an experimenter defines meaning solely in terms of his technique, for he soon finds that he is not communicating with other investigators. The result is a lack of consensus on the definition of meaning (Creelman 1966) which preempts the bid for understanding. The alternative is to de-emphasize the technique, to stress the problem, and to try to see how the results from several methods reflect different aspects of the same underlying capacities.

The differences among the three major techniques that we have used can be expressed in terms of their relative sensitivity to opposites. The free association technique was sensitive only to the relations between antonyms. The free recall technique was clearly more sensitive to such relations than to others, yet did suggest an adult's appreciation of the relations binding other word-pairs. Free recall appears to gauge more distant relations than does free association. The sorting technique most clearly tapped the adult's appreciation of relations among words taken from diverse sections of the lexicon.

Criticisms of the sorting technique that focus on the ambiguity of the instructions are deficient in the way that criticisms of "direct methods" (e.g., Stevens 1957) often are. They fail to note the order in the data. The sorting technique has yielded more orderly and readily interpretable results than the free recall or free association procedures. Sorting has suggested adult sensitivity to features, to equivalence relations, and to the hierarchical structure of the lexicon more clearly than have the other techniques.

There are clearly differences among the experimental tasks. However, there are two reasons for assuming that performance on these tasks may arise from the same type of cognitive capacities. The first reason, on an empirical plane, is that although different results were obtained by the three methods, these results were basically consistent with one another. While the free association technique was sensitive only to the relations binding four word-pairs, it did assign highest proximities to precisely the pairs which received the highest proximities in the other tasks — those comprising antonyms. Moreover, while the level of clustering word-pairs was clearly different in the sorting and free recall tasks, the ordinal relations among proximity values for each were quite consistent, as is evidenced by a comparison of Figures 3.6-3.10 and Figures 4.3-4.7.

The second reason, on a theoretical plane, is that there appears to be one important principle that make sense out of some data from each of the three kinds of tasks. The close correspondence between performance in the last two experiments of the book (i.e., the Bower experiment and, particularly, the Bruner-Olver experiment) and performance in sorting and free recall suggests that clustering in the latter tasks may be mediated by the internal generation of relations making the members of a cluster equivalent. Subjects who cluster words in sorting and free recall may be actively searching for predicates applicable to each of a number of words. Moreover, in our free association data the most commonly given response was the opposite of its stimulus. A preponderance of antonyms or bipolar contrasts in free association has been observed elsewhere (Deese 1962, 1964, 1965). As was pointed out in Chapter 1, the antonymous response violates a theory of free association that is based upon the principle of contiguity, since opposites cannot occur in the same referent at the same time and rarely occur in the same sentences. On the other hand opposites are equivalent along all dimensions except one, and thus nearly any predicate that can be applied to one member of an antonymous pair can be applied to the other. The possible relation between association data and the formation of predicates has been discussed by Miller (1969c), but his emphasis was on associates that occur in the predicates applicable to stimuli, whereas ours is on associates that share the same potential predicates as their stimuli. Presumably both types of relations are operative in different regions of free association norms.

The point behind this speculation is that subjects may group two words into piles, cluster two words in free recall, or associate two words when they can find a predicate that applies to both members of the pair. Although other factors are clearly operative in all tasks, much of the data on the paradigmatic word-pairs that have been presented in this book seem consistent with the 'shared predicate' notion. Such a notion has esthetic appeal in that it unites the different tasks in theory, at least, and in that it relates performance on these abstract and possibly irrelevant experimental games to the pervasive and well-established linguistic ability of producing sentences. If these tasks are viewed as means rather than as ends, as tools for describing the architecture of a net of cognitive capacities, then they can unite in this description in a way that transcends the idiosyncracies of a particular task or a particular method. The free association technique probes the fine structure of highly related words in a semantic space. The free recall and sorting techniques give a broader view of that space.

Combined they produce a picture — rich in structure — of the subjective lexical organization which they are all presumably tapping in some way.

Abstractness

The original definition of abstractness was based upon a set of nested features that were presumed to characterize the relations among the twenty words. If intuition were the sole basis for maintaining the notion, our faith in it might be shaken for the same reason that our faith in the presumed features has been. Subjects see many relations among words that have not been depicted in Figure 1.1. Fortunately, in two sorting experiments the intuitions have been supported. Adult subjects often group words presumed to be concretely related; they seldom group words presumed to be abstractly related.

The result is a shift of emphasis in the notion of degree of abstractness from nested categories to shared features (Miller 1969a). In the case of our set of twenty words these were presumed to be redundant. However, the shift in emphasis allows for verifiability. It also suggests that the relative abstractness for word-pairs can be gauged even when their features cannot be ordered in a nest. Adult sorting behavior conformed, by and large, to the intuitive notion of abstractness. The two cases for which there was not complete conformity were, judging from later analyses, the ones in which our intuitions were possibly most fallible. Since the sorting technique appears to be sensitive to such relations when we think we know them, it might well be applied to words for which such judgment is difficult. The application of the notion of abstractness, which is usually quite restricted (Brown 1958), could be considerably broadened in this way.

The Growth Of Word Meaning

The Concrete-Abstract Progression

Analysis of proximities from the diverse tasks reported in previous chapters results in a picture of lexical growth that has several features of interest. Very young children tend to be idiosyncratic in their organization of words, and when there is uniformity among these subjects it often appears to be the result of what might be called a thematic principle. Adults, on the other hand, are more homogeneous and more often group words that belong to the same conceptual category.

Between these two age extremes there appears to be a gradual transition from one mode of organization to the other which can be described in detail. Locke (1690) appears to have been right. The subjective lexicon is restructured from the ground up. In the two sorting tasks, in the free recall study, and in the Bruner-Olver experiment young children treat words bound by concrete relations as do adults. However, they do not appear to appreciate, as adults do, the more abstract features that relate words, whether this appreciation is reflected in proximities defined by word piles, free recall clusters, or verbalized equivalence relations. There does appear to be a concrete-abstract progression whether such a progression is defined intuitively or empirically. Thus, in spite of the questioning of the notion of a feature, the variability that resulted from using different techniques, and the shift of emphasis in our definition of abstractness, the generalization hypothesis has stood relatively unmarred.

The Lethargy of Semantic Development

Lexical generalization appears to be an extremely gradual process which may never be complete. This lethargy contrasts with the speed of the acquisition of grammar much of which is apparently over when the child is three and one-half or four years of age (McNeill 1968). Although both McNeill (1968) and Vygotsky (1962) have noted the gradual nature of semantic development, neither imagined it to be as slow as we are arguing it is here. For example, McNeill talks of its possible completion when the child is about eight years old. Our studies show that it has only begun at this time.

There has been considerable interest in the fact that the syntagmatic-paradigmatic shift occurs between the ages of five and seven (White 1965). This shift, however, should not be interpreted as a quantal transformation in lexical organization, but, rather, as the important beginning of a process that will continue for many years. The fact that word association results change most dramatically between the ages of five and eight (Entwisle, Forsyth, and Muus 1964) is a product of the technique. The sorting, free recall, and Bruner-Olver experiments show that important events in semantic growth continue at least until an individual has reached college and that not all college students acknowledge very abstract relations such as those that bind the form classes.

Supporting Evidence

Such a description of lexical growth accords with our sorting and free recall results, our version of the Bruner-Olver experiment (as well as theirs [Bruner and Olver 1963, and Greenfield 1966]), our version of the Bower et al. (1969) experiment, some developmental free association data (Woodrow and Lowell 1916) and child vocabulary studies (Brown 1957). It also makes some sense out of other data that on first glance appear puzzling. Our free association experiment suggested that the proportion of paradigmatic responses does not change much in the age groups we were testing. At first the lack of age-related changes in free association might appear inconsistent with the clustering results. However, when the children's associates were examined, as in Chapter 4, it was found that they seemed to bear a specific relation to their stimuli. Many stimulus-response pairs formed bipolar contrasts (Deese 1962). Most of the remaining ones included members belonging to the same specific conceptual category. The words making up these pairs would probably be described by Katz (1966) as sharing several semantic markers. The free association task appears to tap only the kinds of relations that are acknowledged by *both* adults and children in the clustering studies — concrete ones. Thus, the failure to obtain age-related differences in free association is consonant with, indeed predicted by, the generalization hypothesis.

In an analogous case, Steinmetz and Battig (1969) failed to show developmental *changes* in the extent of clustering words belonging to a category although there was considerable clustering at each age level. This might seem to contradict our free recall findings. However, the word clusters they were using would probably be described as concretely related under any definition. The three 4-word clusters were (1) *mother, daddy, sister, brother*; (2) *peanuts, popcorn, candy, gum*; and (3) *dog, cat, horse, cow*. A child's ability to cluster such words in free recall is consistent with the generalization hypothesis.

At the other end of the continuum Cofer and Bruce (1965) found that college students did not cluster words significantly according to form-class in free recall. While this finding is surprising, it becomes somewhat less so when the words of this study are considered. They were taken from three parts of speech (nouns, verbs, and adjectives) so that there was no inter-word associative overlap and so that none of the words within a part of speech were members of a clear cut category other than that defined by form class. According to the present analysis the relations among such words probably stretch the limits of abstractness, and we have seen that even adults often do not acknowledge such relations.[1]

Finally, there is our finding that children from grades 3-4 and grades 7-8 cannot sort the twenty words into the four parts of speech even though the notion of form class is taught in their English lessons from grade 2 on. In the light of the generalization hypothesis this result becomes clearer.

---

[1] Susan Carey and I have used the same words on college students in a sorting task with Miller's usual instructions. We found that some subjects did sort the words according to part of speech, although many did not do so.

Young children cannot grasp the abstract semantic concepts in terms of which parts of speech are taught.

A Remaining Puzzle

In spite of this support for the generalization theory there remains a single but ubiquitous phenomenon that can be viewed as counterevidence. The young child speaks the language and, specifically, the parts of speech are given proper grammatical treatment (Brown 1957; our Frames Experiment, Chapter 5). In a sense this capacity should not surprise us since combining words properly to form sentences suggests a kind of syntagmatic sensitivity which we already knew to exist in children. Nonetheless, within the child's own body of utterances there exists a potential indicant of the most abstract semantic relations among words. These relations could be inferred from distributional similarities. Moreover, in his spontaneous speech the child does treat the members of a grammatical class as equivalent by respecting their privileges of occurrence. How does one reconcile this ability with his apparent inability to treat them as equivalent in our other tasks?

Perhaps there is a parallel here with the discrepant findings of Brown (1957), Brown and Berko (1960), and Werner and Kaplan (1950) described in Chapter 2. Perhaps there is a parallel here also with the finding that use of the rules of grammar in spontaneous speech appears much earlier than the ability to describe those rules. Employing principles and being cognizant of them may reflect very different cognitive capacities. As noted earlier, the close correspondence between performance in the Bruner-Olver experiment and performance in the sorting and free recall tests suggests that clustering in the latter may be mediated by the internal verbal production of shared predicates. In order to generate such equivalence relations an individual must actively and deliberately turn the language upon itself, a feat requiring control and awareness. Viewed in this way the developmental trends reported in this book may be inextricably linked to the growth of an aspect of consciousness.

Bibliography

Anderson, S. W., and W. Beh. The reorganization of verbal memory in childhood. *Journal of Verbal Learning and Verbal Behavior*, 7 (1968), 1049-1053.

Bartlett, F. *Thinking*. New York: Basic Books, 1958.

Bousfield, W. A. The occurrence of clustering in the recall of randomly arranged associates. *Journal of General Psychology*, 49 (1953), 229-240.

———, J. R. Steward, and T. M. Cohen. The use of free associational norms for the prediction of clustering. *Journal of General Psychology*, 70 (1964), 205-214.

Bower, G. H., M. C. Clark, A. M. Lesgold, and D. Wingenz. Hierarchical retrieval schemes in recall of categorized word lists. *Journal of Verbal Learning and Verbal Behavior*, 8 (1969), 323-343.

Brown, R. W. *Words and Things*. Glencoe, Ill.: Free Press, 1958.

———. Linguistic determinism and the part of speech. *Journal of Abnormal and Social Psychology*, 55 (1957), 1-5.

———, and J. Berko. Word association and the acquisition of grammar. *Child Development*, 31 (1960), 1-14.

Bruner, J. S., J. J. Goodnow, and G. A. Austin. *A Study of Thinking*. New York: Wiley, 1956.

———, and R. R. Olver. Development of Equivalence Transformations in Children. In J. C. Wright and J. Kagan (eds.), *Basic Cognitive Processes in Children*. Monograph of the Society for Research in Child Development, 28 (1963), No. 2 (Serial No. 86).

———, R. R. Olver, and P. M. Greenfield. *Studies in Cognitive Growth*. New York: Wiley, 1966.

Carroll, J. D., and J. J. Chang. A new method for dealing with individual differences in multidimensional scaling. Unpublished, 1969.

Cofer, C. N. On some factors in the organizational characteristics of free recall. *American Psychologist*, 20 (1965), 261-272.

———. Some evidence for coding processes derived from clustering in free recall. *Journal of Verbal Learning and Verbal Behavior* 5 (1966) 188-192.

———, and D. R. Bruce. Form-Class as the basis for clustering in the recall of non-associated words. *Journal of Verbal Learning and Verbal Behavior*, 4 (1965) 386-389.

Collins, A. M., and M. R. Quillian. Retrieval time from semantic memory. *Journal of Verbal Learning and Verbal Behavior, 8(2)* (1969), 240-247.

Creelman, Marjorie B. *The experimental investigation of meaning: A review of the literature.* New York: Springer, 1966.

Deese, J. *The Structure of Associations in Language and Thought.* Baltimore: The Johns Hopkins Press, 1965.

———. Form class and the determinants of association. *Journal of Verbal Learning and Verbal Behavior, 1* (1962), 79-84.

———, The associative structure of some common English adjectives. *Journal of Verbal Learning and Verbal Behavior, 3* (1964), 347-357.

Entwistle, D., D. Forsyth, and R. Muus. The syntagmatic-paradigmatic shift in children's word associations. *Journal of Verbal Learning and Verbal Behavior, 3* (1964), 19-29.

Ervin, S. Changes with age in the verbal determinants of word association. *American Journal of Psychology, 74* (1961), 361-372.

Fries, C. C. *The Structure of English.* New York: Harcourt, Brace, 1952.

Gibson, E. J. *Perceptual Learning and Development.* New York: Holt, Rinehart, & Winston, 1969.

Harris, Z. S. Distributional structure. *Word, 10* (1954), 146-162.

Hechinger, G., and F. Hechinger. *The New York Times Guide to New York City Private Schools.* New York: Simon & Schuster, 1968.

Jenkins, J. J., and W. A. Russell. Associative clustering during recall. *Journal of Abnormal and Social Psychology, 47* (1952), 818-821.

Johnson, S. C. Hierarchical clustering schemes. *Psychometrika 32* (1967), 241-254.

———. Metric clustering. Unpublished, 1968.

Katz, J. J. *The Philosophy of Language.* New York: Harper and Row, 1966.

Katz, J. J., and J. A. Fodor. The structure of a semantic theory. *Language 39* (1963), 170-210.

———, and P. M. Postal. *An Integrated Theory of Linguistic Descriptions.* Cambridge, Mass.: M.I.T. Press, 1964.

Kruskal, J. B. Multidimensional scaling by optimizing goodness of fit to a nonmetric hypothesis. *Psychometrika, 29* (1964), 1-27.

Lashley, K. S., and M. Wade. The Pavlovian theory of generalization. *Psychological Review, 53* (1946), 72-87.

Locke, J. *An Essay Concerning Human Understanding.* London: Routledge, 1690.

Mandler, G. Organization and memory. In K. W. Spence and J. T. Spence (eds.), *The Psychology of Learning and Motivation.* Vol. 1. New York: Academic Press, 1967.

———. Association and organization: Facts, fancies, and theories. In T. R. Dixon and D. L. Horton (eds.), *Verbal Behavior and General Behavior Theory.* Englewood Cliffs, N.J.: Prentice-Hall, 1968.

Marshall, G. R. The organization of verbal material in free recall: The effects of patterns of overlap on clustering. Unpublished doctoral dissertation, New York University, 1963.

McNeill, D. A study of word association. *Journal of Verbal Learning and Verbal Behavior, 5* (1966), 548-557.

———. Development of the semantic system. Unpublished, 1968.

Miller, G. A. The magical number seven plus or minus two: Some limits on our capacity for processing information. *Psychological Review, 63* (1956), 81-96. (a)

———. Human memory and the storage of information. *IRE Transactions on Information Theory, 2* (1956), 129-137. (b)

———. Psycholinguistic approaches to the study of communication. In D. L. Arm (ed.), *Journeys in Science: Small Steps – Great Strides.* Albuquerque: University of New Mexico Press, 1967.

――――. A psychological method to investigate verbal concepts. *Journal of Mathematical Psychology*, *6* (1969), 169-191. (a)

――――. Linguistic aspects of cognition: Predication and meaning. In press, 1969. (b)

――――. The organization of lexical memory: Are word associations sufficient? In George A. Talland and Nancy J. Waugh (eds.), *The Pathology of Memory*, New York: Academic Press, 1969. (c)

Osgood, C. E., G. J. Suci, and P. H. Tannenbaum. *The Measurement of Meaning*. Urbana: University of Illinois Press, 1957.

Piaget, J. *The Construction of Reality in the Child*. New York: Basic Books, 1954.

Postman, L. Short-term memory and incidental learning. In A. W. Melton (ed.), *Categories of Human Learning*. New York: Academic Press, 1964, pp. 145-201.

Rinsland, H. D. *A Basic Vocabulary of Elementary School Children*. New York: Macmillan, 1945.

Rothkopf, E. Z., and E. H. Coke. The prediction of free recall from word association measures. *Journal of Experimental Psychology*, *62* (1961), 433-438.

Russell, B. *An Inquiry into Meaning and Truth*. New York: Norton, 1940.

Shepard, R. N. The analysis of proximities: Multidimensional scaling with an unknown distance function. *Psychometrika*, *27* (1962), 125-139, 219-246.

Skinner, B. F. The generic nature of the concepts of stimulus and response. *Journal of General Psychology*, *12* (1935), 40-65.

Steinmetz, J. I., and W. F. Battig. Clustering and priority of the free recall of newly learned items in children. *Developmental Psychology*, *1*, 5 (1969), 503-507.

Stevens, J. C., and L. E. Marks. Cross modality matching of brightness and loudness. *Proceedings of the National Academy of Sciences*, *54* (1965), 407-411.

Stevens, S. S. On the psychophysical law. *Psychological Review*, *64* (1957), 153-181.

Thorndike, E. L., and I. Lorge. *The Teacher's Word Book of 30,000 Words*. New York: Bureau of Publications, Teachers College, Columbia University, 1944.

Tulving, E. Subjective organization in free recall of unrelated words. *Psychological Review*, *69* (1962), 344-354. (a)

――――. The effect of alphabetical subjective organization on memorizing unrelated words. *Canadian Journal of Psychology*, *16* (1962), 185-191. (b)

――――. Theoretical issues in free recall. In T. R. Dixon and D. L. Horton (eds.), *Verbal Behavior and General Behavior Theory*. Englewood Cliffs, N.J.: Prentice-Hall, 1968.

Vygotsky, L. *Thought and Language*. Cambridge, Mass.: M.I.T. Press, 1962.

Watson, J. B., and R. Rayner. Conditioned emotional reactions. *Journal of Experimental Psychology*, *3* (1920), 1-14.

Werner, H., and E. Kaplan. Development of word meaning through verbal context: An experimental study. *Journal of Psychology*, *29* (1950), 251-257.

White, S. H. Evidence for a hierarchical arrangement of learning processes. In L. P. Lipsitt and C. C. Spiker (eds.), *Advances in Child Development and Behavior*. Vol. 2. New York: Academic Press, 1965.

Wittgenstein, L. *Philosophical Investigations*. New York: Macmillan, 1953.

Woodrow, H., and F. Lowell. Children's association frequency tables. *Psychological Monographs*, *22* (1916), No. 97.

Woodworth, R. S. *Experimental Psychology*. New York: Holt, 1938.

Index